Guilty or Innocent?

GUILTY OR

BY ANITA GUSTAFSON

INNOCENT?

HOLT, RINEHART AND WINSTON ▪ *NEW YORK*

Copyright © 1985 by Anita Larsen
All rights reserved, including the right to reproduce
this book or portions thereof in any form.
Published by Holt, Rinehart and Winston,
383 Madison Avenue, New York, New York 10017.
Published simultaneously in Canada by Holt, Rinehart
and Winston of Canada, Limited.

Library of Congress Cataloging in Publication Data
Gustafson, Anita.
Guilty or innocent?
Bibliography: p.
Includes index.
Summary: Examines ten of the most famous
criminal cases in history, juxtaposing two at a time to show
that similar cases may result in different verdicts.
The reader is asked to guess each verdict before it
is revealed.
1. Criminal justice, Administration of—Juvenile
literature.   2. Guilt (Law)—Juvenile literature.
[1. Justice, Administration of.   2. Crime and criminals.
3. Trials]   I. Title.
K5001.G87   1985   345′.05   85-7608

ISBN: 0-03-002927-9

First Edition

Designer: Susan Hood
Printed in the United States of America
10 9 8 7 6 5 4 3 2 1

ISBN 0-03-002927-9

For Cynthia Pope and Dad,
for listening to knee jerks
and remaining friendly

Acknowledgments

I would like to express my warm appreciation for the great help given me by James Cleary, Associate Professor of Law at Drake University. Any infelicities or inaccuracies are mine alone. I also wish to thank journalist Harry Eager and attorney David Hammer for adding a good deal to my knowledge of cannibalism and other forms of mayhem.

Contents

Opening Remarks   1
Cannibalism by the Sea   5
Cannibalism in the High Andes   12
    Places, Laws, Times, and Trials   21
Could a Woman Do That?   26
Could a Foreigner Do That?   40
    When Juries Fail   52
The Body in the Sink   56
The Body in the Parlor   66
    The Body of the Evidence   73
Trial by Media   77
Trial by Mob   89
    How Many Jurors Are Enough?   109
"A Clown Can Get Away with Murder"   111
Can a TV Camera Lie?   122
    The Line Between Insanity and Guilt   135
Summation   139
Bibliography   141
Index   143

Opening Remarks

Do you ever think life isn't fair?

If so, you're right. Because it isn't fair all the time.

For example, suppose you're an average guy in ninth grade, and you've got a little brother, Kevin. A big ninth-grade kid with a name like Dooley Morgerman has been stealing Kevin's lunch money for a month. Pretty soon Kevin is starting to look white-faced and skinny from all those missed lunches and is scared to walk to school alone. You've got other things to worry about and people like Susy Gross-hart to see, but you start walking Kevin to and from school every day anyway. Unfortunately that doesn't work because Dooley just keeps working his oversized extortion racket. You feel dumb about that, and you're also missing Susy.

How do you feel? Angry?

Right. You're furious.

Some people say you see red when you feel this way, but you don't. All you see when you look across the aisle in last-hour biology class is a dark bull's-eye with Dooley's face smack in its center.

Something has to be done about Dooley, you think. You're the one to do it, and today's the day because you've learned that Dooley is terrifying twelve other little kids besides Kevin. Somebody should make *him* hurt—see how he likes it.

1

Well, you will! Right after class.

You study Dooley all through biology class, planning where to hit him first. His stomach, probably. That way you can't miss. It's a big target. But maybe it's too big. You wonder if Dooley will feel a good sharp punch through all that blubber. Will Dooley feel a punch *anywhere*? He's big all over. *Really* big.

You swallow, shake your head. This is no time to think about size.

The bell rings and you stand up. The blood drums in your ears. "Got to talk to you, Dooley," you say.

"Make it fast, wimp," Dooley says. "I'm busy."

Wimp?!

You hit him.

Seconds later Miss Murphy hurls herself into the action. "Stop this!" she shouts. *"Now!"* She hauls you both to Principal Bloom's office. ,

You listen to Miss Murphy tell what happened. You hear Principal Bloom give Dooley after-school detentions for two weeks. Good! you think, and the next minute you're shocked because the principal goes on. "I'm giving you the same detentions," she says.

She stops in astonishment when you jump up and yell "That's not *fair!*"

"What would be fair?" she asks. "You got what you wanted, didn't you? Dooley knows he's going to have to stop taking lunch money from little kids or face stiffer punishment."

She levels a hard look at Dooley, who is studying his ratty Nikes. She turns back to you.

"And you *did* start that fight. If I let you do that for what *you* think is a good reason, I couldn't rightfully stop others from fighting in school for what *they* think are good reasons. Pretty soon, the place would look like a battlefield.''

Put like that, you can see Principal Bloom has to do what she's doing. But it still doesn't seem fair.

Is it fair? You feel that you did the right thing, the moral thing. You saved all those little kids from big dumb Dooley.

Still you can see that Principal Bloom has a point. Smacking Dooley in the hall seemed right, based on your interpretation of right and wrong. Maybe it was. But if everyone walked around the halls hitting people because of what they thought was right or wrong, things would get confusing, if not dangerous.

At a lesser level, Principal Bloom's responsibility is exactly the same as the criminal justice system's. Criminal law is an attempt by the state to preserve public order by making guilty persons liable to punishment, thereby ensuring that private vengeance won't erupt.

In the criminal courts of the United States and other countries around the world, persons accused of violent crimes—felonies like murder, rape, robbery, kidnapping, and so on—are accused by society (not the victim) and are prosecuted by lawyers representing society. They are defended by lawyers representing them as individuals. A *person* can't take the law into his or her own hands; *society* either convicts or acquits the accused through a trial by jury. To convict the accused, a jury must be convinced beyond a reasonable doubt that the person intended to commit a crime and then did it.

Criminal courts are less bloody than the battlefields of war, but they're still battlefields. The weapons are words, evidence, laws. The penalty for conviction is sometimes death. Your confusion about what's fair in the example above is exactly the same problem the jury often faces in a criminal trial. What's fair and right and moral is often in tension with what's actually legal or lawful.

Read on and you become the jury in ten of the most famous, *true* criminal cases in the world. You'll see the facts uncovered by official investigation, and you'll read the arguments heard in court.

You'll have to decide when, if ever, it's all right to eat another person. You'll be asked if *who* you are makes a difference in court. You'll encounter a murder that involved a head of lettuce and a fine watch, and you'll discover a body in a blood-splattered parlor. You'll hear the shouts of a blood-thirsty mob and the nightmare murmurs of the insane.

So observe the evidence; pit your wits against the facts; reach your own conclusions. Decide who is guilty and who is not, then match your suspicions against the verdicts returned by the juries that really had to make these enormous decisions. You may be intrigued by what you read and awed by the jurors' heavy responsibility.

Cannibalism by the Sea

The Chief Magistrate of Glasgow had a problem: People were disappearing without a trace around Galloway.

People had been traveling safely through that rugged area of Scotland for generations. Suddenly now in the early 1600s, people vanished as cleanly and mysteriously as if a monster had snatched them up and tossed them into the sea to wash away with the tide. There was never a clue left. Never a witness.

The magistrate was baffled. Despite the lack of clues, he had to solve the mystery. Most of the people in the area were panicked. And King James VI of Scotland (who was also King James I of England) wanted answers.

So the magistrate's men continued doing what they could —searching the countryside and questioning the people who had last seen a missing person alive.

Some of the people questioned seemed nervous, too ready to claim their innocence. They swore vehemently that they had no idea where the missing person was. Their frantic denials seemed suspicious to the authorities, so some of the people questioned were arrested and some were even executed . . . but the disappearances continued.

Searching the countryside didn't produce anything solid either. It was wild, lonely land, filled with the rhythm of the pounding sea and the cries of gulls. You could ride for a day and see so few people you might as well be alone.

When a party of the magistrate's searchers spotted a cave in the coastal cliffs, they were sure they'd finally hit on something. The cave looked large enough to hide monsters, murderers, or missing persons easily. But when the men saw the high tide fill the cave's mouth, they knew they were wrong. Nothing could survive that drowning rush of seawater twice a day! That search party passed the cave. Later search parties did the same. The disappearances went on.

Years passed. Soon people in the area were even more terrified because shocking *appearances* were added to mysterious disappearances. Severed human arms and legs and lumps of flesh were sometimes discovered washed up on shore or heaped up in a field.

It was obvious to the authorities that there must be some connection between the missing persons and the discarded flesh, but it was hard to say what the connection was. Some of the remains seemed as if they had been salted, dried—preserved, almost as if . . .

The idea was too dreadful to consider, even to people of that era, who were hardened to torture and deprivation. But authorities were forced to look at the facts without revulsion. People were missing. They could have been murdered. Dismembered human remains appeared. The butchered remains had been preserved. Who would butcher and preserve murder victims? People who ate people—cannibals!

The authorities knew they were dealing with something far more sinister than a crazed killer who hacked his victims to pieces in a frenzy. There was a clear, "rational" method used with these remains.

For twenty-five years no one could guess who the cannibal

was, where he sprang from to snatch his victims, *why* he continued. Worse, no one knew why the number of disappearances grew larger each year. Whoever was behind them seemed to have lost control—but not enough to leave a clue or a witness. All authorities could do was keep on searching and hope the marauder made a mistake serious enough to lead them to him.

One night that happened. A woman and her husband were returning on horseback from a nearby fair. A pack of men materialized in front of them and struck, pulling the woman swiftly from her horse. Ruthlessly and expertly they killed her, then moved toward the man.

As he struggled, more attackers spilled from hiding at both sides of the road, and the terrified horses reared, trampling some of the attackers. But that didn't stop the ambush. It was lethally, militarily perfect.

Then, unexpectedly, another group of riders appeared on their way from the fair. They had been wiser than the couple; twenty or more of them rode together. Coming upon the attack, they rushed to help the man. The attackers, now outnumbered, turned and ran. The night hid them as completely as if they had never been there.

But they had. And they'd made several serious errors. They'd left a dead victim, a host of witnesses, and a survivor.

These first solid clues gathered some threads of the mystery. The missing persons were victims of a gang of men and young people, not a lone killer or a monster. Judging from the number of disappearances and the speed with which the gang members vanished, they were people who had lived and operated in the Galloway area a long time. And, judging from the quick, merciless expertise with which they had disemboweled the woman, they were probably cannibals.

The Chief Magistrate of Glasgow listened to the survivor's

report. This was what he'd been waiting for—a break-through! He immediately sent a message to King James, who sent four hundred men and a score of tracker dogs to Galloway, where local people rushed to join the manhunt.

Once again, the area was systematically searched. The cave was noticed, and, once again, everyone believed it was a suicide trap.

The searchers would have passed by the cave this time, too, if the howling, baying dogs hadn't refused to leave. The animals splashed around the mouth of the cave, their actions saying they scented something. Maybe it was only an animal. But maybe it was the cannibal gang! Guards stationed themselves by the cave's mouth. Other men lit torches, drew their swords, and went in.

It was dark a few feet inside the cave, and the men advanced cautiously, following their flickering light. If the cannibals were here, it paid to be careful. The cannibals were experienced killers, and they knew this cave intimately. The searchers were in alien territory.

The men moved through the maze of narrow, twisting passages. They felt the path lead upward, away from the reach of high tide. Suddenly they realized that instead of threatening anyone who hid inside, the high tides were protection!

A mile in, they finally found what they suspected might be there—a slaughterhouse. Strewn about were piles of clothing and jewelry, which had belonged to the victims. In a cavern to one side were heaps of discarded human bones. Before them was the gang.

It was large—forty-eight men, women, and children. They fought, but the outcome was never in doubt. The gang was trapped. Armed men outnumbered them in the cave; armed men waited outside to cut down anyone who escaped. They were arrested, and the king's men heard their story.

The gang was a family. The father, Sawney Beane, had been born to a farming family near Edinburgh. Farming was harder work than Beane wanted. He resented taking orders, and he left home as soon as he could take care of himself, taking with him a young woman who was much like him.

They set up housekeeping in the cave by the sea, thinking it a good home. When the tide was out, there was a fine strip of yellow sand. When the tide was high, only several hundred yards of the cave's main passage was flooded. They could hole up behind those yards of seawater, secure in the knowledge that they would probably never be discovered.

That was important, because Sawney had become a robber, hunting victims on the lonely roads. As long as he took care to leave them dead after he took their money, jewelry, and fine clothing, they could never identify or find him.

But there were big problems with Sawney's plans. One was that he couldn't easily sell the jewelry or clothes for fear they'd be recognized and lead back to him. Another was that most travelers in that part of Scotland didn't carry a lot of money, which he needed to buy food in the area villages. Sometimes the Beanes went hungry.

After the next attack, Sawney dragged the body back to the candlelit cave. He and his wife cut it up and the flesh was dried, salted, pickled, and hung on hooks. The food problem was solved. The money from the robberies could be saved for other necessities.

The Beanes began to have children, and the family went shopping in the villages, spending only what was necessary and not calling attention to themselves. They were so ordinary-looking that they came and went in safety. No one suspected them of being the cause of the terror. But robbery, murder, and cannibalism became routine to the Beanes.

When the Beanes' fourteen children grew up, they intermarried. Soon there was a second generation—eight grand-sons and fourteen granddaughters. A larger family needed more food, so the killings increased. The children were encouraged to help. The family became adept beasts of prey. Sometimes hunting parties of a dozen or more members of the family would ambush and kill groups as large as six men and women.

But soon the Beanes had a new problem. They were such good hunters that they sometimes brought home too much meat. Even though they preserved it, it didn't always last. They discarded what was uneaten in fields or tossed it into the sea far from the cave.

The elder Beanes taught their family that other people were food. That, primitive speech, and hunting tactics were all the younger Beanes needed to know in order to survive. Only two—Sawney and his wife—had ever lived outside the cave, eaten much besides human flesh, or worked at anything other than robbery and murder. The Beane children and grand-children knew nothing except what their parents had taught them; they thought their way of life was normal and right.

After the king's men heard their story, the whole Beane family was marched to Edinburgh. The next day judgment was passed. Sawney Beane and his wife were guilty of murder, robbery, and cannibalism, of course.

But do you think the children and grandchildren were guilty because they participated in the crimes? Or do you think they were innocent because they did not know such behavior was wrong?

· VERDICT ·

The Sawney Beane Family
Found Guilty Without a Trial

Witch burning in the sixteenth century.

All the members of the Sawney Beane family were executed the day after they arrived in Edinburgh. The Beanes were not given a trial because it was decided that their crimes were so dreadful that ordinary law didn't apply. They were outcasts of society and therefore had no rights. The men were executed in much the same manner in which they had killed their victims. After that, the women were burned at the stake like witches.

The Beanes did not protest their innocence or beg for forgiveness despite the fact that they faced violent deaths. Perhaps that was because only Sawney Beane and his wife had any idea that what they had done was a crime.

Cannibalism
in the High Andes

It was 6:00 A.M. on December 21, 1972. Fernando Parrado and Roberto Canessa were awake, anxiously looking over the river that rushed with the southern hemisphere's spring thaw. Would the men they'd seen yesterday and called to for help return?

The day before one of the three men had reined in his horse and shouted "Tomorrow." But there had been so many crushing disappointments. Would this be another, the last before they collapsed and died?

Last night, after they'd seen the men herding cattle to high pasture, the two young men huddled in layers of filthy clothes, too excited to sleep. They were exhausted from their ten-day trek in the icy wasteland of the high, dangerous Andes Mountains, but it was almost dawn before Parrado dropped off to sleep.

Canessa let him sleep past the two-hour watch they'd agreed on. Parrado would need all his strength for tomorrow, especially if the three men didn't return.

But at 6:00 the next morning they had returned! They were there across the river—two men on horseback and a third standing by the campfire!

Parrado ran to the edge of the gorge. The man on foot gestured for him to climb down to the edge of the river before he himself started scrambling for the bank.

Soon only thirty-five feet of cascading, roaring water separated them. Their voices didn't carry over the noise, but the man—a straw-hatted peasant—wrote a note, wrapped it around a stone, and threw it across the river. Parrado stumbled to collect it and read it. It said a man was coming later, and ended with, "Tell me what you want."

Answers must have sprung instantly into Parrado's mind— food, home, to be warm—but there were other steps he had to take before he could have those things.

All he had to write his reply with was a lipstick he'd taken from one of the dead women's handbags. It had kept his lips from splitting in the freezing wind and glaring sun, but as a pen it was almost useless. He signaled, and the Chilean peasant put his ballpoint in a blue-and-white handkerchief, added a stone for weight, wrapped it, and threw the bundle across the river.

"I come from a plane that fell in the mountains," Parrado wrote. "I am Uruguayan. We have been walking for ten days. I have a friend up there who is injured. In the plane there are still fourteen injured people. We have to get out of here quickly and we don't know how. We don't have any food. We are weak. *When* are you going to come and fetch us? Please. We can't even walk. Where are we?"

He added an SOS with the lipstick and threw his note back. The peasant read. Before he waved and left, he pulled a piece of bread from his pocket and tossed it to Parrado.

Bread!

Parrado walked back to Canessa, and the two young men shared it. Several hours later the man the peasant promised would come appeared. His name was Armando Serda, and he was dressed as raggedly as Parrado and Canessa. But he, too, shared the food he carried in his pocket—a lump of cheese. He left to attend to his cattle, promising to return.

Left alone, the two young men ate the cheese. Help had come after so long! They were saved!

Before Serda could return, they buried under a rock the food they'd taken with them from the mountain. They weren't ready for anyone to see the dried scraps of human flesh from the bodies strewn about the shattered plane that had crashed seventy days earlier.

On Friday, the thirteenth of October, the pilot of the Fairchild F-227 had brought the plane down, thinking he was over a pass. Colliding air currents caught the plane and tossed it like a Ping-Pong ball. The plane lost altitude. Its right wing hit a mountain and broke off immediately, tumbling over the fuselage to cut off the tail section.

The vacuum created by the hole in the fuselage pulled out the steward and the navigator, along with the deck of cards they were playing with. Three members of the rugby team that had chartered the plane from the Uruguayan Air Force for their flight to a championship game in Chile were yanked out by the rushing air, still strapped to their seats. The left wing broke away, and a blade of the falling propeller ripped into the fuselage before it disappeared in the deep snow below.

Prayers and screams filled the plane, as what was left of it hurtled toward a mountain. Those not in shock braced themselves to die in the crash.

But the plane surprised them. Instead of crashing into sheer rock, it belly-landed in snow and careered down the steep slope into the valley. As it skidded, two more team members were sucked out the back. Seats torn loose from their mountings by the force of deceleration shot forward.

The plane crashed at 3:30 P.M.; by 6:00 it was almost dark and the temperature was far below freezing. Thirty-two of the forty-five people on board survived the crash to face the first night. Twenty-eight people were alive the next morning, and the team captain, Marcelo Perez, made an inventory of the wrecked Fairchild. No medicine. No emergency supplies or flares. No radio—the batteries were stored in the lost tail section. Liquid: three large bottles of wine, a bottle of whiskey, one of cherry brandy and one of crème de menthe, a half-flask of whiskey. Food: eight bars of chocolate, five bars of nougat, some caramels that had scattered on the floor of the cabin, some scattered dates and dried plums, a package of crackers, two cans of mussels, one can of salted almonds, a small jar each of peach, apple, and blackberry jam.

No one knew when they would be rescued, but everyone thought it wouldn't be long. Still, food and drink were rationed, in case what they had would have to last longer than expected. Perez handed out lunch that day: a square of chocolate and a deodorant-can cap filled with wine for each.

By the fourth day, Adolfo Strauch had discovered a way to get water by melting snow on the aluminum foil from inside the back of a smashed seat. But supplies were dwindling; the freezing nights were threatening.

And no help had come.

That day Parrado and another young man, Carlitos Paez, discussed trekking out, finding their way back to civilization. For the first time, Parrado mentioned cutting meat from the pilots' bodies. Everybody thought he was either joking or mad.

The next day, the fifth day after the crash, the idea sounded saner. Eating the dead might be the only way the living could survive.

By the tenth day, the food shortage was critical and the

prospect of rescue seemed dim. One of the team members wrote: "Today we started to cut up the dead in order to eat them. There is nothing else to do. . . . The bodies are there because God put them there and, since the only thing that matters is the soul, I don't have to feel great remorse; and if the day came and I could save someone with my body, I would gladly do it."

Another team member: "When Christ died he gave his body to us so that we could have spiritual life. My friend has given us his body so that we can have physical life."

By November 1, their twentieth day on the mountain, some of the survivors had died of wounds. An avalanche had claimed the lives of others, including Marcelo Perez. That snowslide had also completely buried those who had died in the crash. Nineteen young men were left, and they had begun leaving a limb or a torso nearby at night in case hostile weather made it impossible for them to reach food. Eating human flesh had become survival. By November 23, even this food source was running low.

It was almost ten weeks after the crash that Parrado and Canessa—the "expeditionary" force nominated to struggle out and bring help for the rest if they could—were saved. One of their first actions was to bury the evidence of how they'd survived. When authorities asked, they told them what had happened at the Fairchild, but omitted details.

"What did you eat?"

Cheese, they said, and herbs they found growing.

When the rest of the survivors were helicoptered to safety, they spoke of cheese and herbs, too. But the mountaineers who flew them to safety snapped photographs of the limbs and bones littering the area around the Fairchild, promising never to publish them.

All sixteen survivors were severely underweight. Parrado

weighed fifty pounds less than normal. Canessa had lost thirty-seven-and-a-half pounds. Thirty, thirty-three, forty-four, eighty pounds—large weight losses in a matter of seventy days, but not large enough for young men who had eaten only cheese and a few herbs and melted snow. Doctors who examined the survivors at St. John of God Hospital in San Fernando, Chile, knew they'd eaten more than they were talking about.

"What was the last thing you ate?" one of the doctors asked casually as he examined the leg of one of the survivors.

"Human flesh," the survivor replied.

The doctor nodded without showing any surprise and went on with his examination. Soon afterward the doctors issued strict orders that reporters and family members be barred from the hospital.

The rescue of the survivors was called the "Christmas Miracle," but the truth of how that miracle had happened was hidden for a time even from the families.

It wasn't easy. Families and friends hadn't given up hoping and searching for the missing rugby players, even though everyone told them no one could live in those barren mountains through one of the worst winters in years. They'd been called mad, but they had harangued and argued and pleaded for yet another search. Now they were anxious for reunion.

The doctors permitted a priest to talk to the survivors, all of whom showed signs of mental disturbance about what they'd done. They wanted to talk away the memory of their cannibalism. They were terrified of being left alone. That was understandable after seventy long days of living packed into the wreckage of the Fairchild's fuselage, sleeping so closely that if someone wanted to roll over, it took a team effort.

The priest assured them that the Catholic Church taught that if it was absolutely necessary to eat human flesh in order to survive, there was no guilt. This brought peace of mind to the survivors who still had doubts about what they'd done, and at last family reunions were permitted.

Families and friends were more shocked at the news than either the doctors or the priest had been, and the families of those who hadn't survived tried hard to understand. But questions from grieving parents were as difficult for the survivors to handle as the anxious days and freezing nights on the mountain had been. How could the survivors explain the mystical sense of friendship that had excused and even encouraged their cannibalism?

Questions from the press were difficult, too. At a press conference held in the next few days, the survivors again claimed to have eaten nothing but cheese and herbs, but the story couldn't be held back. News leaked. The cannibalism story first appeared in a Peruvian newspaper. It was immediately picked up by papers in Argentina, Chile, and Brazil. Reporters swarmed around the survivors, who continued to deny that they had eaten their dead comrades.

On December 26 they could deny it no longer. The Santiago newspaper *El Mercurio* published a picture taken by a helicopter rescuer of a half-eaten human leg lying in the snow beside the Fairchild. Then another Chilean paper printed two pages of photographs, and still another Chilean paper printed the story with a headline: MAY GOD FORGIVE THEM.

The story spread worldwide, but the survivors said they would talk about it only after they were home in Uruguay. Then, they said, they would be judged.

They returned to Uruguay on December 28.

Do you think they were innocent, guilty only of survival? Or were they guilty of a crime so inhuman that society would demand they pay heavily for it?

· VERDICT ·

The Survivors Deemed Not Guilty
Without a Trial

The survivors by the fuselage of the wrecked Fairchild.
(Laffont, Gamma-Liaison)

The sixteen survivors of the plane crash returned to Uruguay and talked, but not in court. Instead, they held a press conference. In the presence of reporters, families, and friends, one of them, Alfredo Delgado, spoke eloquently. He compared their cannibalism to the Roman Catholic Church's rite of Holy Communion.

The press conference ended formal public inquiry. There was no trial, no impaneled jury.

Although some people privately felt the survivors should

have chosen to die rather than survive the way they did, they were a minority. The families of those who hadn't returned supported the actions of those who had. The Church didn't agree with Delgado's comparison of cannibalism with communion, but it said that to resort to "lifeless human bodies in order to survive" was ethically all right. A consensus seemed to be that the sixteen survivors had not committed a crime. Instead, they'd broken a taboo, performed an action society felt was morally wrong.

The "Christmas Miracle" of their rescue didn't solve all the survivors' problems. Even after they were safely home, they showed signs of shock. Many erupted angrily when faced with the slightest frustration. Compulsive, greedy eating was common. So were moody silences followed by compulsive talk about the events on the mountain.

What they had survived was horrible, but the final horror was this: With a little luck, they would have found all the food they needed only five miles to the east of the crashed Fairchild. A hotel was there, closed for winter but stocked with canned food.

Places, Laws, Times, and Trials

Cannibalism is a disturbing subject. Most of us react with horror to homicidal cannibalism. When elderly Albert Fish died in the electric chair for murdering and eating a ten-year-old child in New York in the 1920s, people thought he must be a lunatic. But, lunatic or not, most people thought he deserved his sentence.

Not all cannibalism is regarded with horror. Some scholars seek insight into other cultures by studying the cannibalistic practices of prehistoric—and some modern—warriors, who ate the bodies of their vanquished enemies. By doing this, the warriors believed they would take in the enemy's bravery and, at the same time, keep his spirit from seeking revenge.

Homicide and history aside, most of us shudder when we think of eating another human being, even though enough people were sufficiently intrigued by the idea to make a musical about it, *Sweeney Todd*, a Broadway hit in recent years. But even as we shudder, we wonder if we might not all become cannibals if we had to in order to survive.

Beginning this book with two cases of survival cannibalism (the Beane children, after all, did have to live that life-style if they were to survive) is not as much ghoulish as it is a good opportunity to bring into sharp focus the kinds of tensions societies make laws to resolve.

How does the United States legally view cannibalism? If someone here were brought to trial for survival cannibalism, that person could avail himself of the legal defense of necessity, which goes back to an 1842 case, *U.S.* v. *Holmes*. No one was eaten in this case, but the people in two lifeboats left some ship's passengers aboard the sinking *William Brown*, knowing they would soon die in the icy waters of the Atlantic. Later, people were thrown into the sea to lighten the overloaded lifeboats so that the remaining passengers might survive.

In practice in the United States today, people accused and found guilty of survival cannibalism (often called "desecration of the body" or "disturbing the body") usually escape with light sentences.

Does this mean the United States is soft on cannibalism? Perhaps it means only that there is usually enough food here to keep survival cannibalism from becoming an issue.

But neither the Beane children and grandchildren nor the Andes survivors had any choice—if they wanted to live, they had to become cannibals. Yet the Beanes were killed and the surviving rugby players went free. Is that fair? Maybe the better question is: Is it less wrong to eat other human beings on a mountaintop than by the side of the sea?

That sounds like a silly question, but it isn't. What is *right* changes from place to place. In Scotland in the 1600s, cannibalism was wrong, and the Beanes paid the price. Yet until 1884 and the landmark case *Regina* v. *Dudley and Stephens*, English sailors accepted cannibalism as a cruel but necessary "custom of the sea." Even though it was morally and legally wrong on land, whenever sailors shipped out they knew a disaster like shipwreck could happen, and they knew they could either become cannibals or, in some cases, the victims of cannibals. After that 1884 case, the "custom of the sea" was redefined as murder.

In 1972–73, the South American rugby players remained free, although because their cannibalism didn't seem right to them, they punished themselves emotionally. Yet in 1978, half a decade later, in the starving aftermath of the Cambodian holocaust, a schoolteacher in a refugee camp was reportedly beaten to death as her children watched. She died because she had eaten the body of her dead sister so that she herself could survive.

Place *does* make a difference. Differing societies live in different places, and each *society* decides what is right or wrong. Then those societies—groups of people—set up laws to fit. Laws are nothing but rules that a group of people believes are important. They supply a way to resolve problems that arise in daily life. Few situations are so clear-cut that a person on one side is totally right or completely wrong. Laws attempt to provide guidelines so people can get along reasonably well together.

Laws also evolve with the times. For example, in the United States no one needed laws about automobiles until the 1920s, when many people *had* cars. Laws about privacy are changing right now because so many people own and use computers. Who needed to say manipulating other people's data banks was illegal until there were hackers (people who *could* tap into and manipulate them)?

Our own society's laws change constantly because our society changes all the time. All laws reflect a society's tensions and indecisions, and ours are no different.

The manner in which laws are enforced changes from place to place and from time to time, too. Here, ordinary people sit on criminal juries to decide whether someone is guilty or not guilty of a crime every day. Criminal offenses cover a wide range, from misdemeanors (in which punishment is usually a fine) to felonies (in which the punishment is more often prison . . . or death).

Time and place determine what's immoral or illegal, as the fates of the Beanes and the Andes survivors help show. What seems fair to us today is a result of thousands of decisions and developments made mostly in England and the United States. The past shapes how we think—as a society, as individuals. Our thinking shapes our laws and the way they're enforced.

Our society's tensions and indecisions about something like survival cannibalism reflect our own individual feelings about it, including vengeful outrage, the shock of intrigue, saddened acceptance of necessity. Oddly enough, every law—even dog-leash laws—grew from an initial situation that caused the same kinds of reactions, although they may have been lesser in degree. If something weren't a problem, we wouldn't need a law about it.

And if we didn't have laws, we wouldn't need procedures to enforce them. Serious problems call for serious enforcements, and our jury system is one response.

Neither the Beanes nor the survivors were tried before a formally impaneled jury. Would a jury have decided their fates differently? Perhaps not, yet somehow there is a lingering, "American" feeling that a jury trial would have been "fairer." It's hard to erase the idea that *our* time, place, and methods are right.

Long ago, accused persons could "clear" or "acquit" themselves in other ways, including by their own word or oath. As late as our nation's colonial days, a personal oath was enough to overcome the accusation and testimony of a Native American. The oaths of witnesses could also clear someone in the past. Sometimes whoever rounded up the most witnesses swearing to his innocence won the case—and witnesses were not cross-examined.

Still other old methods of deciding guilt were trials by ordeal or by battle. If an accused person could survive the ordeal of swallowing poison or being burned by fire, he wasn't guilty. If he could beat up his accuser, he wasn't guilty. The "judgment of God" was thought to operate in these trials, and if it kept the accused from death, why should a human interfere?

Here and now persons accused of breaking a criminal law and ordered to appear in court are guaranteed a trial by a jury of their peers—other members of society. But juries have not always tried criminal cases. In fact, that idea emerged only as recently as the thirteenth century in England, on whose legal system much of ours is based. At that time a new method of determining guilt or innocence called inquest gained strength. The "voice of common fame"—what people who knew the accused knew and said about a crime—could put a man in jeopardy. That was the beginning of our private grand jury. But inquest findings couldn't condemn him. That required further consideration, and this was the beginning of our public trial by a jury of peers. By the sixteenth century, accounts of the proceedings of trial juries sound much like ours today. The biggest difference is that there were no defense lawyers then.

How well does our jury system work? Sometimes very well indeed. And sometimes not so well. Read the next two cases and decide for yourself.

Could a Woman Do That?

It was Thursday, August 4, 1892, and the day promised to be as hot and muggy as the day before had been.

At 6:15 A.M. Bridget Sullivan woke. Her attic room in the Borden house at 92 Second Street, Fall River, Massachusetts, was sweltering. She felt ill but she had work to do, so she dragged herself out of bed and down the narrow back stairs.

Her routine was unchanging, but by noon life would be much less ordered and much more terrifying. The events in one of the most famous murder cases in America would occur before then, events familiar to many but mystifying to all. Witnesses' testimony told what had happened that morning.

6:30 A.M.

By now Abby Borden had come downstairs to tell Bridget what to prepare for breakfast. Then she joined John Vinnicum Morse, an overnight guest, in the sitting room. Morse was the oldest brother of Andrew Borden's first wife (Abby was his second), and Andrew relied on him for financial advice. (Lizzie later testified that her father and uncle had sat up late the night before, talking about money in voices that carried and "annoyed" her.)

6:35 A.M.

Andrew came down in a white shirt, black bow tie, and vest. He always dressed in a black woolen suit for business, no matter how hot the day. He placed the key to his locked bedroom on the sitting-room mantel and went out to unlock the barn. He picked up some pears that had fallen from the trees there and brought them into the house. Before he joined his wife and Morse, he washed his face and hands at the kitchen sink. (Andrew was wealthy but his home was small, short on convenience, comfort, and privacy.)

7:00 A.M.

It was 89° already. The Borden daughters didn't eat breakfast with the others. Emma wasn't home, and Lizzie didn't come down. The Bordens felt ill, too, but they ate for an hour, heavy foods like buttered johnnycakes, freshly baked wheat bread, ginger-and-oatmeal cookies with raisins, leftover mutton, leftover mutton soup, coffee with thick cream, fruit.

8:00 A.M.

With breakfast over, Abby told Bridget to wash the windows. She herself started dusting the first floor, while Andrew and Morse relaxed in the sitting room.

8:40 A.M.

Morse stood, saying he would walk to visit some family a mile and a half away. Abby reminded him of dinner; he promised to be back by noon. Andrew went with him to unlock the kitchen doors, stepping outside to talk privately with him. Bridget heard their lowered voices as she washed the dishes. Andrew called, "Come back to dinner, John," before he reentered, relocked the door, and prepared for his day as usual. He brushed his teeth at the sink, took his bedroom key from the mantel, drew a basin of water for his washstand, climbed the back stairs.

9:00 A.M.

Lizzie descended the front stairs, stopped to speak with Abby, came to the kitchen to make herself coffee. When Andrew came down, Lizzie gave him a letter to Emma and asked him to mail it. Bridget's queasy stomach revolted then, and she dashed to the backyard. When she returned, Abby was waiting in the dining room to remind her to wash the windows. Andrew had left. Lizzie was gone, probably back upstairs in her room.

9:30 A.M.

Abby went up the front stairs to tidy the room in which John Morse slept. Bridget never saw her alive again.

10:45 A.M.

Bridget had finished washing the windows in the sitting room. She still felt rotten. She decided to go to her room and lie down. The front doorbell stopped her. She answered it, surprised to find someone had locked the door and thrown the bolt as well. That wasn't unusual at night, but this was broad daylight! "Oh, pshaw!" she said, annoyed. She heard someone laugh at the top of the stairs, and she turned. It was Lizzie.

And it was Andrew at the door, carrying a roll of papers. Lizzie came down. She mentioned that Abby had gone out in answer to a note from a sick person. Andrew was surprised. It was hot and his wife hadn't been feeling well herself. He didn't either. He took the key from the mantel, went up the back stairs to his bedroom, came down a short while later to nap in the sitting room.

Bridget decided against her nap. She took her window-washing ladder and basin into the dining room, where Lizzie was ironing handkerchiefs. Lizzie asked Bridget if she planned to go out. Bridget said she didn't know; she felt ill. Lizzie ironed as Bridget finished the windows and took her gear into the kitchen. When she returned, Lizzie told her about a sale of dress fabric. Bridget said, "I am going to have one," but the nap would come before she bought the material to make a new dress. She trudged up the back stairs to her room to lie down. She heard the City Hall bell ring. An hour until noon.

11:00 A.M.

Next door, Adelaide Churchill left her house to buy groceries. On her way home, she saw Bridget rushing home white-faced from Dr. Bowen's house across the street and wondered if someone was sick at the Bordens'.

Once inside her kitchen, she looked from her window at the Bordens' back door. Ten yards away Lizzie leaned behind the screen door, holding her head, and with an excited, upset expression. Mrs. Churchill called, "Lizzie, what is the matter?"

Lizzie turned, as if startled. "Oh, Mrs. Churchill, please come over! Someone has killed Father!"

Minutes later, Mrs. Churchill had come around the four-foot-high fence separating the two houses. She asked Lizzie where her father was and pushed open the door to the sitting room. (Later, at the trial, a prosecuting attorney would detail Andrew's ten head wounds, illustrating his words on a plaster cast of the old man's skull.) Andrew's wounds were still fresh when Mrs. Churchill saw him, but she didn't take time to count slashes. She glanced, gasped, and returned to the kitchen.

"Where were you when it happened?" she asked Lizzie.

"I was in the barn. . . . I went there to get a piece of iron."

"Where is your mother?"

Quietly, Lizzie said, "I don't know. . . . She got a note to go see someone who is sick." Then Lizzie asked for a doctor, saying Dr. Bowen wasn't home.

Mrs. Churchill ran to find her hired man and tell him to

fetch another nearby physician. A news dealer overheard her. When she left he phoned the *Fall River Globe* to give them the exclusive on a "knife slashing."

11:15 A.M.

The news dealer called the police.

Dr. Bowen was already there when Mrs. Churchill got back, asking for a sheet to cover Andrew's body. Bridget knew where the linens were kept, but she was terrified to get them alone. The killer might be lurking. Mrs. Churchill went with her to Andrew's and Abby's bedroom to get a sheet. When he'd covered Andrew, Dr. Bowen left to send a telegram to Emma. Mrs. Churchill again asked Lizzie where her mother was.

"I wish someone would try to find her. I thought I heard her come in," Lizzie said.

Since Bridget was still frightened, Mrs. Churchill again went with her, this time up the front stairs. Moments later Mrs. Churchill was back, sitting at the kitchen table, her hands shaking. "She's up there," she said.

Dr. Bowen returned and learned of the discovery of Abby's body. He climbed the front stairs to the guest room. Abby lay in a pool of blood, her head nearly separated from her body. The blood from her nineteen blows was dark and congealed. She'd died before her husband.

There was no sign of struggle anywhere. Even the fringed bedspread Abby had been smoothing was still in place, un-wrinkled. The killer had surprised both victims and vanished, moving unseen and unheard through the small house at 92 Second Street that had no privacy but many locked doors.

There were few clues in the case—so few that Andrew's and Abby's funeral was interrupted so police could collect their heads for the evidence contained in the slashes. And in-quest testimony and other evidence was confusing.

When Bridget was questioned at the inquest, she was terrified *she* would be arrested. All she could add to what she'd already told authorities was that the Borden household was unhappy and tense. Andrew had begun locking his and Abby's bedroom because in the last year, Abby's trinkets had been stolen and their room ransacked. Andrew thought someone in the house was responsible. But Bridget had no motive to murder Andrew and Abby Borden. She said she stayed on only because Abby begged her to.

Emma had a motive. She'd resented Abby since the woman married her father thirty years ago when she was nine and Lizzie two. Her ill feeling had grown lately when Andrew gave his wife a farm, land that Emma thought should belong to her and Lizzie. Andrew gave his daughters gifts of equal value, but the gift to his wife rankled, and the thought that there might be more was alarming. Morse's financial advice might end in Andrew's making a will . . . and it might favor Abby. But Emma couldn't have committed the murders. She had an alibi: She was visiting friends in another town when they occurred.

No one checked her alibi, but they looked into John Morse's. It was watertight. The relatives he'd been visiting at the time of the murders firmly supported it.

Lizzie had no alibis other than her own statements, and unfortunately for her, her statements changed each time she made one, at, before, and after the inquest. Sometimes she said she was in the barn during the time of the murders. Once she said she went there to get material to repair a screen, other times for iron to make sinkers for her fish line, and still other times to eat pears. She also said she'd been eating pears under a tree or had been in her room mending lace during the time in question.

Her confusion at the inquest could have been caused by

being forced to create an alibi on the spur of the moment. It could have been an attempt to "cover up" for someone else. (Books have been written "proving" Bridget's or Emma's guilt.) Or it could have been the effect of morphine prescribed by her doctor to ease the horror of her father's death. (They were close. When a child, she'd given him her small, gold ring as a bond; he was buried wearing it.)

Whatever the source of Lizzie's confusion, the authorities had none. They knew she'd been as upset as Emma about Andrew's gift to Abby. They knew she'd tried to buy deadly prussic acid the day before the murders, supposedly to use in cleaning a sealskin coat. (Prussic acid couldn't be used for that and the druggist hadn't sold it to Lizzie, but the attempt to buy it showed murderous intent.) They knew she'd been at home during the ninety minutes in which the murders were committed, even though she claimed not to have heard anything unusual. They'd checked the loft of the barn and found thick dust undisturbed on its floor. And they'd found several axes in the house, including one with a freshly broken handle. The axe head was covered with ashes, as if someone had tried to disguise that it had been washed.

Lizzie's defense attorney was barred from the inquest. Under Massachusetts law a prosecutor could choose to hold an inquiry before a judge, and a suspect didn't have the right to be represented by counsel. Witnesses could be sworn and both the judge and the prosecutor had the right to question them.

At the end of the third day, August 11, Lizzie Borden was charged with the murders and arrested. The next morning a preliminary hearing was set for August 22.

In Lizzie Borden's preliminary hearing, two of the major issues that would later collide at her trial surfaced. One argued for her innocence in the murders. An expert had tested all the axes and hatchets found in the Borden basement. He had discovered no traces of blood on any of them. The gray hairs adhering to one had come from a cow. Without an easily and rapidly hidden murder weapon, the prosecution's success in convicting Lizzie would be hampered. She hadn't had either the time or the opportunity to get rid of a weapon off the premises.

The other major issue dealt in a less evidential way with the likelihood of Lizzie Borden's guilt. She was a woman, and the society of the time found it difficult to believe a woman could murder her parents. Judge Blaisdell thought a woman could. He said, "Suppose for a single moment a *man* was standing there. He was found close by the guest chamber, which to Mrs. Borden was a chamber of death. Suppose a *man* had been found in the vicinity of Mrs. Borden—was the first to find the body—and the only account he could give was the unreasonable one that he was out in the barn looking for sinkers—then he was out in the yard—then he was out for something else—would there be any question in the minds of men what should be done with such *a man?*" He decided Lizzie was "probably guilty" and sent her to the grand jury.

The grand jury's job is to inquire and investigate behind closed doors. The grand jury decides if the accused should be ordered to stand trial (indicted). Indicted persons are then arraigned, or ordered to appear in court, to be identified, hear the charges against them, and plead guilty or not guilty. They are tried before a petit jury. (*Petit* is a French word meaning small.) The "small" jury is made up of people drawn by lot from a list of voters. It listens to evidence from witnesses, then decides whether to release (acquit) a person being tried (the defendant) or convict him or her. When the grand jury that would decide whether Lizzie Borden should go to trial convened in November, it listened to evidence for two weeks without an indictment. But on December 1, the grand jury reconvened to hear a witness testify about a dress.

Lizzie had burned the dress she'd worn during the crucial ninety minutes because it had brown paint stains. Brown is the color of dried blood. The grand jury decided it was high time Lizzie appeared before a petit jury.

Her trial began on June 5, 1893. A panel of three Superior Court judges presided because Massachusetts law required such a panel in cases where a verdict of guilty meant death. One hundred and eight possible jurors were questioned before twelve were chosen.

The prosecution's case against Lizzie was based on her confused testimony at the inquest, the burned dress, and the broken-handled axe—the murder weapon, they said. Its cutting edge fit the Bordens' wounds exactly.

Lizzie's defense managed to strike the testimony of the three inquest witnesses who knew about the prussic-acid episode. The jury couldn't use any of this information when deciding on its verdict. Emma testified she had suggested that Lizzie burn the dress. And the defense demolished the credibility of the broken-handled axe as the murder weapon.

The defense went further, producing witnesses who said they had been in the barn's loft *after* the time that Lizzie said she'd been there. If the dust on the floor wasn't disturbed, perhaps police investigators hadn't looked carefully enough. Other defense witnesses described strange people seen lurking around the Borden house. Still more witnesses testified as to Lizzie's churchgoing, Sunday-school-teacher character.

The defense noted that it didn't have the burden of proof. It didn't have to prove who *had* murdered the Bordens, only that Lizzie couldn't have. Lizzie, said the defense, was innocent. A woman couldn't do such a thing. A guilty verdict would result in her death in the electric chair. "You are trying a capital case," the defense attorney said, "a case that involves a human life, a verdict in which against her calls for the imposition of but one penalty, and that is that she shall walk to her death." The defense thus clarified the jury's hard decision—set Lizzie Borden free or execute her.

The prosecution's closing arguments hit hard on the idea that somebody in the house had to have committed the murders. It was locked inside and out, right down to the closet at the head of the stairs and the barn door. On the day of the murders, the front door was locked and bolted. Because there were no halls in the house and each room had to be entered either from the back or front stairs or from another room, it was highly improbable that a stranger could scuttle through, hide, and vanish.

Woman of good character or not, there were excellent reasons why Lizzie wanted her parents dead. A woman was physically able to kill them with an axe, and such a woman would not be stopped by "feminine" emotion. "They are no better than we," the prosecution said. "They are no worse than we. If they lack in strength and coarseness and vigor, they make up for it in cunning, in dispatch, in celerity, in ferocity. If their loves are stronger and more enduring than those of men, on the other hand, their hates are more undying, more unyielding, more persistent." Contrary to what the defense claimed, a woman could do this; Lizzie was guilty beyond a reasonable doubt.

On June 20, 1893, the case went to the jury after one of the judges charged them. "You have listened with attention to the evidence in this case and to the arguments of the defendant's counsel. It now remains for me, acting in behalf of the court, to give you such aid towards a proper performance of your duty," he said.

He went on to destroy the prosecution's case. He mentioned again Lizzie's fine character, to excuse her confused statements as to her whereabouts when the murders were committed, to urge the jury to ignore what they read in the newspapers and seek only the truth. If they could do that, he said, the trial would "express in its results somewhat of that justice with which God governs the world."

With that remarkable and partisan charge ringing in their ears, the jury took only an hour and six minutes to bring in a verdict.

What do you think? Was Lizzie Borden guilty? Or was she innocent of the crime and guilty only of being in the wrong place at the wrong time?

· VERDICT ·

Lizzie Borden
Found Not Guilty

Lizzie Borden. Could a woman commit the crime?
*(Photograph courtesy of the
Fall River Historical Society)*

"*Not guilty*," the jury foreman said.

Lizzie sank into her chair and covered her face with her hands. Spectators in the courtroom cheered and waved their hats and handkerchiefs. People lined up to shake her hand and murmur "God bless you." They held up babies for her to kiss. They'd read the newspapers, and they shared the popular view: "A woman couldn't do such a thing."

She and Emma returned to a banker's house in Fall River. Guests poured into the house, crowds gathered outside, and shortly after 10:00 a band arrived. People inside and out sang "Auld Lang Syne."

Even though Lizzie had testified that Andrew had left a will, none was found. She and Emma inherited a fortune. They bought a large house in the best section of town and named it Maplecroft. But not long after the "outsider" newspeople left, townspeople who had supported Lizzie during the trial ostracized her. No new suspect was found, and the townspeople began to wonder about Lizzie's innocence.

Three years after she was acquitted of murder, Lizzie shoplifted two porcelain paintings from an art gallery. The gallery owner threatened to take her to court unless she "confessed" to the murders. He said he just wanted to know the truth and promised to keep the confession secret.

Perhaps Lizzie dreaded another imprisonment. She went to a nearby typewriter and wrote: "Unfair means force my signature here admitting the act of August 4, 1892, as mine alone."

Legal experts who later studied the records of the case conclude that Lizzie's typed "confession" was the truth. They say the trial was conducted unfairly. When one of the three presiding judges instructed the jury, he said that there was no direct evidence and that a respectable woman like Lizzie couldn't have killed her parents. When Lizzie's inquest testimony and that of the three prussic-acid witnesses was barred, the jury was almost forced to acquit. Evidence was suppressed or incorrectly stated by the defense. Some Fall River residents felt some witnesses helped Lizzie simply because she was one of them.

Following a quarrel with Lizzie, Emma moved from Maplecroft, and the two never spoke again. But Emma firmly believed in her sister's innocence. Twenty years after the trial she said, "If Lizzie had done that deed, she could never have hidden the instrument of death so that the police would never find it."

The case is still unsolved.

Could a Foreigner Do That?

Midafternoon of April 15, 1920, five men staged a payroll robbery at a shoe factory in South Braintree, Massachusetts. It was a smooth, professional job. Two employees—a paymaster and his guard—were killed, and the bandits escaped with $15,776.

Witnesses later described the car. It was "newly painted" and "shiny" to some; "dirty," "old," and "unwashed" to others. They agreed that it was large and dark-colored, however, and that the bandits were "foreign-looking."

Authorities immediately asked garage owners in the metropolitan area south of Boston to notify police if any foreigners tried to obtain an automobile. They were especially interested in foreigners who behaved suspiciously.

Three weeks later, four Italian men arrived at Simon Johnson's garage in Bridgewater, wanting to pick up a stored 1914 Overland. It was owned by one of them, a man named Boda. The Italians didn't get the car that evening because Johnson pointed out it needed a new license number. While they were there, Mrs. Johnson went to a neighbor's house and phoned the police.

As she returned home she saw two of the men leave on the

motorcycle and side car in which they'd arrived. The other two men, whom she later identified as Nicola Sacco and Bartolomeo Vanzetti, watched her before they walked away.

That night a Brockton police officer approached Sacco and Vanzetti as they rode a street car. Vanzetti, who spoke with an accent, later testified about what happened: "The officer who arrested me on the electric car come in the front of the car and walked toward the back of the car, and when he come near the chair where we sit down, I and Sacco, he say, 'Where do you come from?' And we answered, 'We come from Bridgewater.' Then he took out a revolver. He pointed to us a revolver at me, yes, sir, and say, 'You don't move, you dirty thing.'"

Sacco and Vanzetti were arrested and searched by Brockton police. Both men were armed. Sacco carried a fully loaded Colt automatic pistol, .32 caliber, and there were additional cartridges in his pocket. Vanzetti had a loaded .38 Harrington & Richardson revolver, but no extra ammunition. The two were taken to the Brockton police station and booked.

Vanzetti testified that he asked the Brockton police why they had been arrested. "They say, 'Oh, you know, you know why.' And when I try to sleep in the cell, there is no blanket, only the wood. Then we called for the blanket, because it was rather cool. They say, 'Never mind, you catch warm by and by, and tomorrow morning we put you in a line in the hall between the chairs and we shoot you.'"

Sacco and Vanzetti had been seized without warning and imprisoned without being told the charges against them. These violations of their constitutional rights weren't unusual at the time—especially if you looked foreign or spoke accented English.

Not long after the Communist revolution in Russia in 1917, the United States was in the grip of a "deportation delirium." Communist organizations had sprouted in America; some bombs had been mailed to public officials; buildings had been blown up and the terrorists were foreigners. The Attorney General warned that sixty thousand dangerous alien radicals roamed the streets. It was believed that the aliens (also called "Communists," "anarchists," "Bolsheviki," "reds," "radicals") wanted to overthrow the American government.

To combat this, Justice Department agents infiltrated the membership of Communist and socialist organizations in preparation to raid and catch radicals so they could be deported—sent back to the countries from which they'd come. Once the undercover agents were in place, they could make sure meetings were scheduled for the night of the big raid, January 2, 1920. They did.

On the night after the new year, police swept in on meetings in homes, offices, lodge halls, union headquarters, and churches in thirty-three cities and towns across the nation. They arrested three thousand men and women believed to be part of the conspiracy. Smaller raids followed for nearly a year, and some of the people arrested were held in prison for months without being charged or told why they were being held.

Some newspapers applauded the arrests, saying America was being made safe for Americans. Other newspapers wondered what had happened to the right of free speech guaranteed by the U.S. Constitution. The "make America safe for Americans" newspapers countered that aliens didn't have constitutional rights. They weren't citizens of the United States. They were only visiting, and they weren't good guests.

Lawyers working for the release of one small group of the imprisoned people petitioned federal Judge George W. Anderson. In a decision handed down on June 23, 1920, Judge Anderson said that aliens living in the United States did have constitutional rights, including the freedom from unreasonable search and seizure and from arrest without due process of law. "A mob is a mob," he wrote, "whether made up of government officials acting under instructions from the Department of Justice, or of criminals, loafers, and the vicious classes."

The judge found that the arrests had been illegal, the proceedings irregular throughout, and the imprisonments without trial unlawful. He freed that group of "reds."

Other "Communists" weren't so lucky. On May 3, 1920, Andrea Salsedo jumped or fell to his death from a prison window in New York City. Headlines read: RED'S DEATH PLUNGE, 14 STORIES, BARES LONG BOMB TRAIL. Jumped? Fell? Or pushed? Salsedo's friends wondered.

Among them was Vanzetti, an immigrant from Italy and a fishmonger. Sacco, younger than Vanzetti, had also emigrated from Italy, supporting his family at the time of his arrest by edge-trimming soles in a shoe factory.

Both were politically active. Vanzetti often spoke on street corners about the shocking difference between the lives of the rich and poor in the United States. Both had run to Mexico to avoid serving in the American army. Both lied following their arrest: Sacco claimed he didn't know Boda; Vanzetti claimed his revolver cost $19, later $5. Neither had been swept up in the raids, but both were indicted by a grand jury in September 1920 for the murder of the two shoe-factory employees. A date was set for their trial in Norfolk County.

Starting on May 31, 1921, seven hundred citizens of Norfolk County were summoned and questioned. A jury of twelve was chosen early in the afternoon of June 4 and sworn in by Judge Webster Thayer.

The trial that followed produced thousands of pages of transcripts and crowds of eyewitnesses and experts. Frederick G. Katzmann led the prosecution. The state's case depended in part on Sacco's absence from work on the day of the crime, in part on the "consciously guilty" behavior Sacco and Vanzetti exhibited following their arrest, as shown by their lies. And there were other points as well.

In his opening remarks to the jury, Katzmann promised to present eyewitnesses who said they'd seen Sacco and Vanzetti at the robbery and had identified them from photographs or from seeing them in the Brockton police station. He said the getaway car was a Buick, stolen by the defendants and found abandoned in the woods near the scene of the crime. He said he'd tell how they used the car in the murderous robbery. He said he'd produce the cap Sacco lost when he committed the crime. He said the state's experts would prove that the bullet that killed one of the two victims came from the gun Sacco had stolen from one of the dead men and still carried when he was arrested.

That's the "story in the rough," Katzmann said in conclusion to the jurors. When they heard the witnesses and had their evidence, he asserted they would agree that Sacco and Vanzetti were guilty even though they pleaded not guilty. "Very likely," he added, "it will be a long trial."

He was right. He might have added the trial would be confusing, because it was that, too.

When the defense cross-examined one witness who had testified before the grand jury, she wasn't positive she'd seen

Sacco; she was sure before the petit jury. That witness per-jured her earlier testimony, and so did other witnesses. One, Lola Andrews, fainted on the stand when the differences in her testimony became too complicated to keep track of.

The defense also called eyewitnesses. Some testified that they'd seen Vanzetti busy peddling fish far from the scene of the murder on April 15. Some said they'd seen Sacco in Boston at the time of the crime.

The prosecution produced the cap left at the scene of the robbery, claiming it was hard evidence that tied Sacco to the murders. Katzmann made much of a hole in the cap, which he said was made by Sacco's habit of hanging the cap on a nail while indoors. Sacco's defense asked him to try on the cap, and Sacco did. It was a size 6⅞. Sacco's hat size was 7⅛. The hat was much too small and obviously did not belong to Sacco.

The prosecution brought a ballistics expert to the stand to testify about the murder bullet. When a bullet is fired, the gun leaves marks on it that are as individual and unique as a per-son's fingerprints. The testimony of the state's expert left the impression that the marks on the bullets at the scene of the crime were consistent with having been shot from the gun in Sacco's possession. The defense offered their own ballistics experts, who said the bullet couldn't have come from Sacco's gun.

The prosecution asked the defendants why they had wanted Boda's car from the Johnsons' garage. Vanzetti said they needed it to collect radical literature from their friends' homes so they wouldn't be caught with it in a raid. Fear of deportation and memory of Salsedo's death had led him to ask for the use of the car. In fact, that was the same reason he and Sacco had lied to authorities when arrested—they were protecting their friends. That was why they left the car there when Johnson said Boda's car needed new license plates.

Nonsense, the prosecution said. They left the car there because they'd seen Mrs. Johnson leave and were afraid she'd call the police. They had stolen a car earlier, knew all about the robbery and murders at South Braintree, and knew they were guilty. The lies they told after arrest and their actions in running from the Johnsons' garage were caused by their consciousness—awareness—of guilt.

Six weeks after it had begun, the murder trial was over. The evidence was in, Judge Thayer made his charge to the jury, and the jury left to make its decision.

Sacco and Vanzetti were proven liars and radicals, involved in attempts to change the U.S. government. But were they also guilty of robbery and murder?

· VERDICT ·

Nicola Sacco and Bartolomeo Vanzetti
Found Guilty of Murder in the First Degree, July 14, 1921;
Pardoned, July 19, 1977

Vanzetti (*left with mustache*) and Sacco arriving at court for
sentencing.   *(National Archives)*

The jury was quick. Both Sacco and Vanzetti were equally guilty. The foreman gave the verdicts, and Sacco shouted, "They kill innocent men. They kill two innocent men."

A long series of appeals was filed as new evidence came to light. Intellectuals the world over, labor leaders, poets, novelists, artists, members of the most aristocratic families in Massachusetts, some of the most prestigious lawyers in the country, and everyday workers assailed the trial. Felix Frankfurter, Sherwood Anderson, H. G. Wells, Alfred Dreyfus, Edna St. Vincent Millay, John Dos Passos, Upton Sinclair, Sinclair Lewis, Maxwell Anderson, Albert Einstein, Thomas Mann, John Galsworthy—a fair listing of the brightest and the best of the times, and all of them protested. So did thousands of "nameless" people who saw the mob Judge Anderson had spoken of earlier run wild.

The protesters had questions. Who were the other three bandits in the car? What happened to the $15,776? None of it was ever traced to Sacco and Vanzetti's families. They were poor and would surely have used it. How were Sacco and Vanzetti—a factory worker and a fishmonger—able to pull off a perfectly timed crime? They didn't have the expertise! They were simply blue-collar workingmen with a dream. The most violent they became was to talk on street corners, trying to make life better for their families. The most dishonest they were was to lie in an attempt to protect their friends.

These were excellent questions. In addition, the honesty of jury, judge, and prosecution was suspect. Consider:

- Judge Thayer was quoted as saying that they'd finally gotten those "anarchist bastards."
- The foreman of the jury had told a friend that whether

Sacco and Vanzetti were guilty or not, they should get what was coming to them as radicals.

• One of the prosecution's ballistics experts said that the prosecution's questions were phrased so that they made him say exactly the opposite of what he meant. He'd been given no chance to explain his misleading answer.

• Lola Andrews, the fainting eyewitness, retracted her identification.

• A Morelli gang member named Medeiros confessed to the South Braintree crimes. In prison at the time, his first confession was sent to a newspaper, intercepted by authorities, and suppressed. His second confession, delivered directly to Sacco, matched other information suppressed by authorities. Because Medeiros's confession mentioned two cars, murky questions about timing and car identification were suddenly clear.

None of the appeals were accepted. Under Massachusetts law then in effect, appeals for a new trial had to be heard by the original trial judge—Thayer. He denied them all. Felix Frankfurter, a Supreme Court justice, noted that in denying the appeals, Thayer referred to testimony that wasn't even in the record! Much evidence had been suppressed by the prosecution in cooperation with the judge.

And much of that suppressed evidence would surface much too late to help Sacco and Vanzetti. In 1969 Herbert B. Ehrmann, the last living lawyer to have been associated with the defense, wrote a book showing that the prosecution's suppression of evidence extended even to fingerprints taken from the getaway car!

On April 9, 1927, Thayer sentenced Sacco and Vanzetti to die in the electric chair. The two were given an opportunity to speak. Sacco said he was innocent, accused Judge Thayer of full knowledge of that fact, and expressed his appreciation for the support of intellectuals and his comrades of the working class. Vanzetti was eloquent:

> I am not only innocent of these two crimes, but in all my life I have never stolen and I have never killed and I have never spilled blood. . . . I am suffering because I am a radical and indeed I am a radical; I have suffered because I was an Italian, and indeed I am an Italian; I have suffered more for my family and for my beloved than for myself; but I am so convinced to be right that you can only kill me once but if you could execute me two times, and if I could be reborn two other times, I would live again to do what I have done already.

Sacco and Vanzetti were electrocuted on August 23, 1927. Thousands joined the funeral procession for the eight-mile journey across Boston. Thousands of others lined the streets to look on.

Before he was executed, Vanzetti said:

> If it had not been for these thing, I might have live out my life talking at street corners to scorning men. I might have die, unmarked, unknown, a failure. Now we are not a failure. This is our career and our triumph. Never in our full life could we hope to do such work for tolerance, for justice, for man's understanding of man as now we do by accident. Our words—our lives—our pains—nothing! The taking of our lives—lives of a good shoemaker and a poor

fish-peddler—all! That last moment belongs to us—
that agony is our triumph.

On July 19, 1977, fifty years later, the governor of Massachusetts granted Sacco and Vanzetti a posthumous pardon. He said, "Any remaining stigma should be removed from their names." Sacco and Vanzetti were exonerated of all guilt in the South Braintree robbery and murders.

They were, however, a long time dead.

When Juries Fail

The criminal justice system in the United States is like a hockey game, in which words and evidence are the puck. The prosecution, representing society, smashes words around, attempting to establish the guilt of the accused beyond a reasonable doubt. The defense smashes words back in an attempt to make the jury doubt. The judge is the referee. The accused sits around like somebody who didn't get picked when sides were chosen and tries not to do or say anything self-incriminating. In fact, the accused has the *right* not to say anything at all, and the jury isn't supposed to wonder why.

This is called the adversary system of justice, and sometimes it's a bad game.

After the Sacco and Vanzetti trial, questions arose. Is the adversary system fair? Do we give a convicted person adequate opportunity to appeal for a new trial? Is the testimony of experts handled wisely? Are there adequate safeguards against judges' abuse of their power?

Those questions arose partly because of the judge's statement about getting the "anarchist bastards," which indicated he'd decided Sacco and Vanzetti were guilty before the jury said they were. In the United States, an accused person is assumed to be innocent until proven guilty. Another reason those questions came up is that the prosecution hid evidence—suppressed it. Because the accused is assumed to be innocent, the prosecution bears the burden of proof of guilt in a criminal case. But this doesn't mean they can either hide or make up facts. When the defense doesn't know all the facts, it can't bring them out in court . . . and the jury can decide only on the facts they hear there.

Society's substitutes—the prosecution—and the referee judge didn't play fair in the Sacco and Vanzetti trial. They won, but they won dirty.

Questions also arose after the Lizzie Borden trial. Lizzie's defense managed to suppress facts that may have convicted her. In this trial, too, the judge overstepped his authority. In his charge to the jury, he said a woman couldn't have murdered her parents with an axe.

The defense and the judge didn't play fair in this trial either. They won, but they won dirty.

A jury's decision is only as good as the information it rests on, but trial lawyers aren't always interested in playing fair. The applause of winning the case can overcome their desire to seek justice. Then, too, attorneys are advocates of their clients, not necessarily of the truth.

And a jury's decision is only as good as the individual jurors' motives, too. The foreman in the Sacco and Vanzetti case wasn't playing fair when he said that even if the two were innocent, they should be convicted because they were "reds."

Our adversary system, another inheritance from English law, works only if *everybody* is honest.

Is there a better way? Some countries have modified the procedure. Since 1933, English and Welsh courts have moved from impaneling a jury except where it is required—in criminal cases if the accused pleads not guilty to an indictable offense. Since the 1960s, unanimity of the jury's vote is also not required. And there are other systems. Many European and Latin American countries follow a system based on Roman law, which relies on the judge.

In the Roman system, evidence is gathered by the defense attorney and the people's attorney, who isn't considered a prosecutor. They spread every true fact in the case they know before the judge, who digests it all. Then the judge questions and cross-examines the witnesses. In this system, a trial is a fact-finding expedition rather than an attempt to convict or defend the accused. That may sound more fair than our "hockey game" until another major difference between this system and ours is considered—the accused is not presumed innocent until proved guilty. In the Roman system, the accused is guilty until adjudged innocent.

Something is gained or lost in any legal system, and ours tries to shore up its weaknesses. One way it does this is the manner in which new evidence discovered after the jury's verdict is in is handled. If the accused is acquitted, he or she can't be put in double jeopardy (tried a second time for the same offense). That's why Lizzie Borden's typed "confession" in the art gallery couldn't have been used against her. A jury's verdict of not guilty is final, even if new evidence strongly indicates guilt. But a jury's verdict of guilty is *not* final. A convicted person may appeal it to a higher court. Appeals are attempts to protect the accused.

Other protections arise from the judge. A verdict of guilty can be set aside if the judge believes it's contrary to law. This may lead to a new trial in some states; in other states and in federal courts, a judge can acquit defendants no matter what the jury says.

Even with these safeguards, *who* you are can determine guilt. As is obvious from the cases of Lizzie Borden and Sacco and Vanzetti, inequalities in income, social standing, educational background, national origin, and sex can be reflected in the courts. Lizzie Borden was deemed incapable of the murders because she was a good, churchgoing woman. Sacco and Vanzetti were deemed capable of their crime because their backgrounds were less savory.

Until 1963, a poor man or woman could be tried without a defense, and a sexual prejudice is shown today in that laws about juvenile delinquency are often harsher on girls than boys. Girls with a record of running away are more likely to be sent to a training school or other correctional institution than runaway boys, who are often not punished at all, according to E. B. Fincher in *The American Legal System.*

The positive way to look at these inequalities is to see them as motivation to continue the struggle for equal justice. The negative way is to assume they're right and ignore them. Always, the best way to avoid inequalities in any given case is for the jury to look closely at the evidence—which isn't always easy, as the next two cases show.

The Body in the Sink

D r. George Parkman was in a hurry. He always was, especially on the way to a business appointment. He strode briskly from his home in Boston, leading with his large jaw full of badly fitting false teeth. It was said Parkman was so impatient he'd hop off a horse if he thought he could make better time afoot.

Today, his jaw thrust abruptly into Holland's Grocery store at about 1:45. He ordered thirty-two pounds of crushed sugar and six pounds of butter and said to send it out this afternoon. He dropped off a paper bag, said he'd pick it up later, and left, heading off toward Harvard.

When Parkman didn't hurry back for his paper bag, grocer Holland opened it. It contained lettuce.

Parkman didn't hurry home that night either. Dinner wasn't the same without him and his lettuce. It would never be the same again—but not because of the lack of lettuce. Dr. Parkman himself had disappeared.

Two days later the papers carried a notice saying Parkman was last seen "in the southerly part of the city, in and near Washington street, in conversation with some persons, at about five o'clock of the afternoon of" November 23, 1849. The ad invited anyone with information to share it with the

Boston City Marshal, "for which he shall be liberally rewarded."

Maybe if this ad had mentioned the lettuce and said it was for Parkman's invalid daughter, someone would have answered. Maybe not. In any case, no information came. Parkman's brother-in-law tried again with another ad the next morning.

$3,000 Reward

DR. GEORGE PARKMAN, a well-known citizen of Boston, left his residence, No. 8 Walnut street, on Friday last. He is sixty years of age, about five feet, nine inches high; gray hair, thin face, with a scar under his chin; light complexion, and usually walks very fast. He was dressed in a dark frockcoat, dark pantaloons, purple silk vest, with dark figured black stock, and black hat.

As he may have wandered from home in consequence of some sudden aberration of mind, being perfectly well when he left his house; or, as he had with him a large sum of money, he may have been foully dealt with. The above reward will be paid, for information which will lead to his discovery, if alive; or, for the detection and conviction of the perpetrators, if any injury may have been done to him.

A suitable reward will be paid for the discovery of his body.

BOSTON, November 26th, 1849
Information may be given to the City Marshal.

Someone answered this ad. Marshal Tukey received a letter postmarked Boston and signed CAPT OF THE DARTS. The captain said Dr. Parkman had been murdered and gave the location of the body. But there was no trace of Parkman there, so the next day's ad targeted different prospects—jewelry lovers.

$100 reward will be paid for Information which leads to the recovery of a gold double-bottomed lepine turned casewatch, ladies' size, full plate, four-holed jewelled, gold dial, black figures, steel hands, no second hands, no cap. Marked F. B. Adams and Sons, St. John street, London. No. 61,351.

FRANCIS TUKEY, *City Marshal*
Police Office, City Hall

Talking of watches had no more pulling power than the earlier ads. No one responded with information about the watch.

The next day, Parkman's brother-in-law offered $1,000 for the recovery of the doctor's body, "as fears are entertained that he has been murdered," but it wasn't until after the thirtieth that the ads brought in anything like the desired response. Then, *two* letters came to Marshal Tukey, both mailed on the same day, November 30. One, a red envelope postmarked East Cambridge, contained this interesting information, but no signature:

Mr. Tukey
    Boston
    Dr. Parkman was took on Bord the ship herculan and this is al I dare to say or I shal be kiled.

Est Cambrge one of the men give me his watch
but I was feard to keep it and throwd it in the water
rightside the road to the long bridge to Boston.

The other, mailed in Boston, was signed CIVIS. This letter
said the police should try searching East Cambridge cellars,
although CIVIS felt Parkman's body was probably "cut up
and placed in a stout bag, containing heavy weights, and
thrown off one of the bridges."

By now there was talk. Murder, of course, is always more
interesting than either fine watches or discarded lettuce. And
Dr. Parkman's possible murder was more interesting than the
average homicide because Parkman himself was more interesting than average.

Although he was a physician, Parkman's practice was business and finance. He loaned money happily, then ferociously
nagged his debtors to repay. Some called him threatening.
Strangely enough, he was also generous with his profits. He
had established the Parkman Chair in anatomy and phys-
iology at Harvard and had financed the building of the
school's new Medical College.

Parkman was a philanthropist skinflint, and he believed in
punctuality. Before he left home the Friday he disappeared, a
visitor had come to arrange a business appointment at 1:30.
Parkman had been running late that day—he didn't leave
Holland's Grocery before 1:45. Perhaps that was why he
seemed especially rushed. He hadn't mentioned where that
meeting was or with whom, but his family thought he must
have disappeared at or after it.

The more people talked about Parkman's disappearance,
the more some of them remembered seeing the man shortly
before 2:00 that day at the Medical College. Those eyewitnesses seemed more solid than the letters sent to Marshal

Tukey. But whom had Dr. Parkman been in such a rush to meet? Somebody in the Medical College?

Those questions were easily answered. On the Sunday afternoon after his uncle's disappearance, Parkman's nephew stood near the Medical College talking with police. Dr. John White Webster walked up and shook his hand, saying he'd just read Parkman was missing in the papers. He went on to identify himself as the person Parkman had been rushing to meet. In fact, he said, they *had* met, and Webster had paid a $483 debt he owed Parkman. Then the missing man had dashed to East Cambridge to pay a mortgage Webster owed. Webster said he'd trusted Parkman with the deed because "we all know Dr. Parkman to be an honest man."

That sounded like bad business practice to Parkman's nephew, but who could doubt Webster's word? The professor was an eminent member of the Harvard faculty. He held a Master of Arts and a Doctor of Medicine, was a member of several prestigious academic societies, had written several books, was Erving Professor of Chemistry and Mineralogy. Besides, the man seemed so sincere. Later that afternoon, he even went to the missing man's brother to pay his respects.

But there was another side to Webster, a side guaranteed to set businessman Parkman's false teeth on edge. Webster was a spendthrift. He often invited students home, entertaining them and other guests lavishly. He'd inherited $50,000 from his father, but building a large house in Cambridge and entertaining soon took care of that.

Harvard paid him only $1,200 a year; it wasn't enough. In 1842, Parkman had loaned him $400 to tide him over. In 1847, Parkman joined a group of men who gave Webster more money. In return for $2,432, Parkman took a mortgage on all Webster's property. That money lasted a year. A short time later, Webster arranged another loan, this time from Parkman's brother-in-law. He used his cabinet of minerals as collateral. Unfortunately, Parkman already owned the minerals. When this news came out in family conversation, Parkman was shocked.

As soon as possible, he stomped jaw-first to the Medical College to talk business with Webster. A janitor, Ephraim Littlefield, overheard parts of the tense conversation. Parkman wanted Webster to pay him something on account. Webster said he couldn't at the moment, but he promised to do something about it by the next day, November 19.

Webster ignored his date with Parkman, so the doctor came to see him on the twentieth. Parkman strongly urged Webster to make a payment soon or he'd bring the entire affair into the open. That's why Webster had called on the twenty-third to set up the meeting that afternoon.

Janitor Littlefield didn't know what happened at the last meeting, but he knew Webster began to act strangely after it. For one thing, he offered to buy the Littlefields' Thanksgiving turkey, and he'd never done that before! Then, too, he came to work early the day before Thanksgiving, and there were mysterious sounds behind his blocked keyhole. That afternoon, Littlefield touched the wall outside Webster's assay furnace. The furnace was used to analyze the mineral contents of rocks, so it was often hot. But today it was blistering, much hotter than usual.

Littlefield decided to investigate. When Webster left he locked the doors, but that didn't stop Littlefield. The janitor climbed in through a window and found bones in the furnace and wet acid on the floor.

By a week after Dr. Parkman's disappearance, Littlefield

had investigated further. He'd knocked a hole in the thick brick wall of the professor's privy and looked through it to make an astonishing discovery: Under the water splashing into the professor's sink were a man's pelvis and two parts of a leg! Said Littlefield, "I knew that it was no place for these things." He notified authorities.

Shortly thereafter, authorities notified Professor John White Webster that he was charged with the murder of Dr. Parkman. Webster swallowed a dose of strychnine on the way to the police station but recovered. He was fit and healthy when he was brought to trial in March 1850.

All the seats in the courtroom were claimed by privileged spectators, many of whom thought Webster was innocent. After all, the professor often dissected people, mostly criminals who had been hanged.

A lot of other Bostonians believed in his innocence, too. And even if they didn't, they wanted to attend the trial. Police hospitably and quietly moved groups of spectators in and out of the galleries every ten minutes. Around sixty thousand members of the general public were thus accommodated during the eleven days of the trial.

The prosecution relied heavily on Littlefield's testimony about the quarrel and Webster's strange goings-on. The state also produced evidence that Webster had been juggling his financial records. Fragments of false teeth found in the furnace were entered into evidence, and so were larger parts of a human body found in the tea chest Webster kept in his laboratory. But all this evidence was circumstantial. No one had seen Webster kill Parkman, although the circumstances seemed to indicate he had.

The defense noted the lack of direct evidence. It asked if the human bits were really Parkman's. It suggested that even if they were, someone else might have put them there to incriminate Webster, perhaps someone like Littlefield. It produced eyewitnesses who had seen Parkman later on that Friday in other parts of the city. Unfortunately, the eyewitnesses had mistaken either the date or the man.

Then dentist Dr. Nathan Keep, a friend of both Webster's and Parkman's, took the stand. He'd made Parkman's false teeth, and the fragments in Webster's furnace fit his molds exactly.

The jury listened to Chief Justice Lemuel Shaw's evenhanded and intelligent summation of the law. Look at the evidence as you reach your verdict, the judge told the jury. You must be satisfied either that Webster murdered Parkman or that he ordered someone else to do it. If you're not satisfied beyond a reasonable doubt, acquit Webster . . . but keep in mind that a person's good character can't override strongly proven facts.

The jury was out for three hours. At 11:15 that night, they returned to announce their verdict.

Do you find the facts strong enough to convict Webster? Or do you think he should have been acquitted?

· VERDICT ·

Professor John White Webster
Found Guilty

Dr. Webster killing Dr. Parkman in the laboratory.
*(Courtesy of the New-York Historical
Society, New York City)*

Although he was found guilty, many people still believed in Webster's innocence. Webster appealed the verdict in a long letter to Governor Briggs. He said he was "entirely innocent of this awful crime," and he claimed to be a "victim of circumstances, or a foul conspiracy, or of the attempt of some individual to cause suspicion to fall upon me."

But a couple of weeks later he wrote a confession, admitting the murder but saying it wasn't premeditated (he hadn't planned it). Parkman came to the meeting in such a furious mood that he drove Webster to snatch up a stick and smash him over the head. Parkman died with that one blow.

Webster said he burned Parkman's clothes, cut up his body and began burning that, and dropped the doctor's watch into the river. He'd written the three letters to Marshal Tukey, hoping to keep the law busy until he could dispose of every bit of Parkman.

Webster was hanged on Friday, August 30, 1850.

The Body in the Parlor

Insurance agent William Herbert Wallace of Liverpool, England, was a very calm, quiet man, who came home one freezing January evening in 1931 to find his wife very dead.

He didn't know she was dead at first. In fact, he didn't even know if he could get into the house. Both the front and back doors were bolted. Some neighbors came out to watch him, and they advised him to try the back door again. When he did, it opened.

A dim light burned in the kitchen. Wallace softly called his wife's name. "Julia? Julia?"

There was no answer.

Wallace climbed upstairs. Julia wasn't in either bedroom. He came downstairs and went to the door of the front parlor.

"Julia?"

No answer.

Wallace stood on the threshold and struck a match. With the help of its flickering light, Wallace finally found his wife.

She was neatly laid out on the parlor floor, her feet near a gas burner in the fireplace. The fire wasn't lit, but Julia's skirt was partly burned. So was the tail of a rolled-up raincoat tucked under her shoulders. Obviously the burner *had* been lit earlier in the evening. That was unusual; the couple seldom used this room.

Now everything in it, including Julia, was bloody—the gas burner, the sofa cushions, the hearth rug, the walls and ceiling and chandelier. Someone had beaten Julia to death with a heavy, blunt instrument.

Wallace quietly called the neighbors. He led them to the parlor, then out again. When police arrived, he was sitting in a rocking chair, stroking his black cat. He looked at them calmly through his gold-rimmed glasses and told them what he knew.

At 6:05 that night he had come home for tea. Julia was alive then, and she was alive when he left at 6:45.

Later, witnesses would testify that Wallace had indeed been dealing with his insurance business at 5:55 on Eastman Road. The boy who delivered milk saw Mrs. Wallace alive at 6:30, although it may actually have been a bit later than he said. When police reconstructed his route, they found he would have arrived at the Wallaces' home at 6:31 or perhaps two or three minutes later. These minutes are important.

Wallace told police he left home that night to answer a message left at his chess club by a R. M. Qualtrough the night before. To the person at the club who had taken the message, Qualtrough's voice sounded distant but happy. It was his daughter's birthday, he said, and he wanted to buy an insurance policy. Would Wallace please come to his home at 25 Menlove Gardens East the next night?

Wallace tried to. He was seen boarding a tram two miles from his home at 7:06. Nine minutes later, he was seen boarding another tram heading for the Menlove Gardens area. At 7:45, he asked directions from a police constable. At 7:52 he was seen studying a street directory in a newspaper shop. He was having problems finding Qualtrough's house.

There was a perfectly good reason for that. There was no street in Liverpool called Menlove Gardens East. Menlove Gardens West, North, and South existed, but Menlove Gardens East did not. Wallace gave up his search and came home, arriving there at 8:45 to find Julia dead in the parlor.

Police questioned Wallace for days. They tried to shake the man's story, especially after the pathologist estimated the time of death at nearer 6:00 P.M. than 7:00. This ignored the milk-boy's evidence, but it put Wallace in the house with the victim. It also gave him plenty of time to wash off the blood spatters before he left the house to meet Qualtrough.

The problem was this: If the milk-boy saw Mrs. Wallace alive at 6:30, Wallace would have had to murder her and get cleaned up *fast*. The latest he could have left home to catch the tram he was seen on was 6:49. At most he would have had nineteen minutes. Was that enough time to bludgeon his wife furiously, lay her out neatly, remove every trace of blood from himself, and walk calmly to the tram?

Wallace was arrested and charged with his wife's murder. Throughout the questioning and the trial, he remained calm and soft-spoken. His story never changed, and the case has become a classic one involving circumstantial evidence. Look at the evidence from one point of view, and Wallace was guilty. Look at it from the other, and Wallace was not.

From the prosecution's point of view, Qualtrough's phone call was a lie. Wallace himself made the call, disguising his voice and leaving a phony message in order to establish an alibi. This idea was supported because telephone engineers were able to trace the call to a pay phone only four hundred yards from Wallace's house. The call was made at the time Wallace would have passed it walking to the chess club the night before his wife died.

The prosecution based its view of the murder on Wallace's expertise at chess. He planned his wife's murder in the same methodical way. He arrived home at 6:05 the night of the crime, said the prosecution. Then he went upstairs, saying he was going to change for his meeting with Qualtrough. Instead he stripped and put on the raincoat. He came downstairs to the parlor and called his wife. She came into the dark room, he beat her to death, and then laid her out. Growing cold in his raincoat, he lit the gas burner. Julia's skirt caught fire, and he smothered the flames with his coat. He folded it and placed it beneath her body. Then he went upstairs, bathed, and went out to "find" the nonexistent Qualtrough. While out, he threw away the murder weapon—a fifteen-inch iron rod a cleaning woman said was missing from the parlor. He took great care to be seen roaming around looking for an address he knew was impossible to find.

The prosecution had no idea why Wallace killed his wife, but calm people have been known to erupt in murderous furies. And Wallace had the time to do so. The prosecution pointed to the pathologist's estimate of the time of death. Here's what a scientist thinks, they said. Will you believe a scientist or a boy delivering milk?

The defense looked at these same facts from another point of view. Yes, the call from Qualtrough was a fake. And yes, it had been made from a booth near Wallace's home. But that argued in favor of Wallace's innocence. If a cunning chess player were planning a murder, he wouldn't use that phone. The true murderer would, however, because that would throw suspicion on Wallace. The defense noted that the waitress who took the message at the chess club didn't recognize the voice. The fake phone call was a way to get Wallace out of the house the next night so the real murderer could get in.

The defense turned to the pathologist's time-of-death estimate. Not only did it fly in the face of the milk-boy's eyewitness report, but it was also nonsense. The pathologist based his estimate on how rigid the victim's limbs were. This stiffness, called rigor mortis, occurs on a regular timetable after a person dies. However the progression of rigor mortis changes due to outside conditions—delayed by cold, hastened by heat. Taken by itself, rigor mortis is not a reliable guide to establishing the time of death, and the pathologist had taken rigor mortis by itself, ignoring other important measurements. The pathologist was wrong; Julia Wallace was alive shortly before her husband left, just as the milk-boy claimed. And it simply wasn't possible that Wallace could have beaten his wife, fought a fire, bathed, dressed, and left in minutes.

There was no reason to suspect Wallace of the murder. He had never been accused—even suspected—of anything illegal in the past. Murder was out of character for him, and he'd had no reason to slaughter his wife. They were happy, and there was only a tiny insurance policy on her life. Wallace stood to gain absolutely nothing with her death except a long, lonely life.

The defense reminded the jury that it didn't have to decide who killed Julia Wallace. The jury had only one thing to decide in this trial: Was it certain beyond a reasonable doubt that Wallace had done it?

The four-day trial ended. The jury took one hour to reach a decision.

How do you look at this case—from the prosecution's point of view or that of the defense?

· VERDICT ·

William Herbert Wallace
Found Guilty and Sentenced to Death;
Found Not Guilty by a Court of Criminal Appeal

Reginald Gordon Parry. Did
he kill Julia Wallace?

The Wallace case made legal history in Britain when a
Court of Criminal Appeal overturned the jury's conviction on
the grounds that the verdict wasn't supported by evidence.
There was ample room to doubt Wallace's guilt.

Wallace was freed, and he retired to a small farm outside
Liverpool. He lived alone, keeping guns handy and his house
fortified with a system of lights and burglar alarms, fearful

71

someone would come and kill him as they had Julia. Two years later, he died of natural causes.

The case is still officially unsolved, but evidence indicating a possible murderer surfaced publicly fifty years after Wallace's trial. Radio reporters in Liverpool interviewed an elderly witness, who repeated what he'd told police in 1931 during their investigation of the case.

Early in the morning after Julia Wallace died, a young insurance agent brought his car to be cleaned in the all-night garage where the witness, John Parks, worked. The young man, Reginald Gordon Parry, was visibly upset, and his car was bloody. Parks found a bloodstained glove, and Parry snatched it from him, saying, "If the police found that it would hang me." He also blurted out that he'd dropped an iron bar down a street grating.

Parry and Wallace had worked for the same insurance company until Wallace discovered money missing from the collection fund. Parry was fired, a possible grudge motive for the murder. Parry had an alibi for the night of the murder. He said he was with his girlfriend. At first she said that was true; later she said it wasn't.

Parry is now also dead of natural causes.

The Body of the Evidence

All the facts surrounding dead bodies found in sinks and parlors—or ditches, for that matter—is evidence. Since the end of the 1600s, when the jury was deemed to have no information to use in arriving at a verdict other than what they heard in court, evidence has come from the testimony of witnesses. Even real, or "physical," evidence like the revolver used in a murder must be identified as the murder weapon through the testimony of witnesses before the revolver can become an exhibit.

When the body of evidence from both the prosecution and the defense is complete, it becomes proof. It establishes a fact. Either the accused is guilty as charged or innocent for all time of the alleged crime.

It's obvious that in order for a trial to be fair, the evidence the jury considers must be fair. Rules of evidence that help ensure this were developed, and keep developing. They change when old rules are no longer workable, when new rules are added to adapt to new situations, with court decisions and federal or state laws.

Some evidence, like information obtained through wiretapping (listening in to the phone conversations of others when they don't know it), is inadmissible in court. When a lawyer jumps from his chair during the questioning of a witness and shouts, "Objection!" he's often objecting to the fact that inadmissible evidence is about to be brought in, and he's asking the judge to decide if that is the case.

Lawyers can object to questions on other grounds, too, and

some evidence is excluded before it even surfaces in court. Evidence that would destroy a relationship like that between husband and wife is excluded because it's felt that some relationships are more vital to society's well-being than having all the evidence presented in court. Also excluded is evidence that may prejudice the jury too much against the defendant. For example, certain photographs may not be admitted into evidence if their emotional impact might prejudice the jury. The criminal record of the accused may be excluded for the same reason, and evidence that violates the accused's constitutional rights is also excluded, as it is unreliable evidence, like hearsay: "I didn't see it myself, but somebody told me. . . ."

So much information about an accused person and the case can be kept from the jury that the rules of evidence seem overly restrictive to some authorities. But the aim is to protect the rights of the person on trial and to further ensure that a trial is played fair.

To help make sure that what witnesses say under oath—the testimony—is exactly what they meant to say, no more and no less, opposing attorneys can cross-examine them. This helps weed out errors, lies, misstatements. And to help the judge make sure that a trial proceeds in an orderly way, evidence is presented in a traditional pattern.

Evidence may be documentary—anything written, like the ransom note in a kidnapping case. It may be real, "physical" evidence like a revolver. The testimony of experts provides opinion, which is added to the body of evidence. It may be corroborating evidence, which supplements and strengthens evidence already given, or cumulative evidence, which merely repeats what has gone before.

It may be direct evidence—an eyewitness saying he saw the

accused stab the victim—or it may be circumstantial evidence. The classic example of circumstantial evidence is the footprint Robinson Crusoe saw in the sand on the island on which he was cast away. From this he inferred that there was another person currently on the island.

In law, circumstantial evidence involves inferring from accepted facts, facts that are still at issue. In other words, if enough facts are known, facts that aren't known can be reasonably guessed at. When that body was found in Dr. Webster's sink, it was a fact. What was known of Webster's and Parkman's characters and relationship were facts. So when the false teeth in the furnace were proved to be Dr. Parkman's, it was reasonable to infer that the body in the sink was his, too. Which, of course, the jury did. (So, by the way, did the dentist who made those teeth. He wept on the witness stand because he knew he'd just consigned Webster to death.)

Which is better in court—direct evidence or circumstantial evidence?

Neither. And both.

Few murderers or kidnappers invite people to watch them killing or snatching their victims. Violence is usually done in private, so direct evidence in criminal cases like the ones in this book is hard to come by.

Chief Justice Shaw referred to this in his charge to the jury in the Webster case. He asked, "But suppose no person was present on the occasion of the death . . . is it wholly unsusceptible of legal proof?" His question was rhetorical, because he already knew the answer. If the facts of the circumstances linked up so overwhelmingly that no reasonable person could come to any other reasonable conclusion, it was proof of guilt.

A strong chain of circumstantial evidence can be compelling to a jury and so can direct, eyewitness evidence. Eyewitnesses, however, are often untrustworthy, as this experiment shows:

A professor of criminology taught a class of police officers, lawyers, and law students. His students were intelligent and more-or-less trained observers. But when a stranger waving a pistol burst into the classroom in the midst of a lecture, fired at the professor's chest, and dashed away as the professor crumbled, the students were stunned. The students did not know that the professor had staged the event. No bullets were fired. But the experiment proved the professor's point. The eyewitness descriptions of the stranger would have given police severe headaches if the case had been real. Descriptions of hair color ranged from black to blond, height varied as much as twelve inches, and weight by fifty pounds. Some students said the stranger was German, others said Italian, two said Oriental.

Because of experiments like this, the value of some direct evidence has been questioned. Because of cases like Wallace's, circumstantial evidence can also raise uncertainties. Good lawyers and judges help juries base their decisions on a solidly forged chain of all types of evidence.

When evidence is mishandled, bizarre and astonishing verdicts can occur, as in the two disquieting cases that follow.

Trial by Media

E arly on the morning of July 4, 1954, Mrs. Marilyn Sheppard was murdered in Bay Village, Ohio.

The killer did a thorough job. Bits of her teeth were broken in the attack. The bedroom walls were spattered with blood. A trail of stains led down the stairs to the first floor of the suburban Cleveland house. She screamed loudly enough to wake her husband, Dr. Sam Sheppard, who was downstairs. He'd fallen asleep there earlier while watching TV and after talking with visitors.

It had begun as a pleasant evening. The Sheppards, members of a wealthy, influential family in the area, had surprised their friends with news of a new baby. They both seemed pleased and excited. When the other couple left after midnight, they saw Marilyn lock the door leading to the lake in front, but didn't notice if she also locked the door leading to the road.

A few hours later screams shocked Dr. Sheppard awake.

He dashed upstairs. The dressing-room light he usually left on only when he was out on call dimly illuminated the house. He saw a large white figure standing over Marilyn's bed before he was knocked down—"clobbered," he said.

Sometime later he revived, heard noises in the house, then

saw the white form running down the lawn to the beach house. He chased and caught it, fighting long enough before he was knocked down again to know it was a burly man with bushy hair.

When he came to this time, he was lying partly in the water. Dazed, he staggered back to the house, went up to his wife, felt for her pulse. There wasn't one. He phoned a friend, John Spencer Houk. "For God's sake, Spen," he said, "get over here quick. I think they've killed Marilyn."

When Houk and his wife arrived minutes later, the door facing the road was unlocked. Inside, Houk stumbled over Sheppard's medical bag, which was lying in the hallway, and looked up to see Sheppard slumped in a chair in the den.

He wore no shirt, his trousers were dripping wet, and there were discolored, swollen spots on his face. He groaned, obviously dazed, and explained what had happened, as Mrs. Houk ran upstairs. She came down, crying, "Call the police, call an ambulance, call everything!"

Sam Sheppard's brother, Dr. Richard Sheppard, arrived at 6:10 A.M., soon after the first policeman. Richard went upstairs, thinking he could help Marilyn. He couldn't. He estimated she'd been dead for no more than two hours.

Richard's hands were bloody from the examination. When he went to the bathroom to wash them, he noticed a non-filtered cigarette butt floating in the toilet and was surprised. His brother didn't smoke. Marilyn smoked once in a while, but only filtered cigarettes. He left the room without realizing the cigarette butt could be a valuable clue.

Back downstairs, he found Sam lying on his back, now apparently in great pain. Sam's rumpled sport jacket was lying on the floor beside the couch.

"Did you have anything to do with this?" Richard asked in a low voice.

"Hell, no."

The two continued talking quietly.

At 6:20, the suburban police chief and Dr. Stephen Sheppard, another brother, arrived. Sam repeated his story, in such pain now that Stephen thought the blows from the bushy-haired man might have injured his spinal cord. He took Sam to the hospital, one owned and operated by the Sheppard family, where nurses noted his skin looked as if it had been in water a long time. Two of his teeth were broken.

Meanwhile, Richard woke seven-year-old Chip, who was still sleeping soundly in his second-floor bedroom, and placed him in his wife's care, as police searched the house. Drawers had been pulled open and objects scattered. Marilyn could have been killed by a burglar as Sam said . . . but windows and doors showed no traces of breaking and entering.

Coroner Samuel R. Gerber arrived at 8:00 A.M. Some time before then, someone had neatly folded Sam's corduroy jacket and placed it on the couch. Someone had drawn down Marilyn's pajama top, thus changing the position of her arms, and a policeman had flushed the toilet, thereby destroying the cigarette butt.

Gerber learned that Stephen Sheppard had taken his brother to the hospital. He heard that Richard Sheppard had asked Sam if he had anything to do with the murder. And he began to suspect that he knew who the murderer was.

He went to the hospital. Sam now wore a neck brace, but he didn't look badly injured to Gerber. He asked that Sam's clothes be turned over to him and was surprised when there was no shirt. Sam said he'd been wearing a T-shirt but didn't know what had happened to it. Gerber was suspicious about this, and he was curious about a bloodstain on the knee of Sheppard's still-wet pants. Sam said he must have picked it up when he knelt on the bed to check his wife's pulse.

Gerber returned to the house. Investigators had found a boat bag holding a bloodstained wristwatch that had stopped at 4:15 A.M., Sheppard's old fraternity ring, and a key ring. Gerber thought this evidence could have been planted to support Sam's burglary story. He took no fingerprints from these objects. He couldn't take any from the house because everything had been wiped clean. It even looked as if someone had tried to clean up the trail of blood leading between floors.

On the underside of Marilyn's pillow, Gerber found a huge bloodstain. He stared at it, ignoring the spatters on the walls. It looked to Gerber like the imprint of a clamplike, double-pronged surgical instrument. Although he didn't recognize its shape, he knew Sheppard had many instruments. When he learned that Sheppard had been seen with another woman, he was sure Sheppard had murdered his wife so that he could be with her.

Asked about the woman later, Sam denied it—several times. Gerber knew Sheppard was lying about this, and he thought Sheppard was lying about the other things, too, although his story never changed.

Gerber set about accumulating evidence for a conviction. He had tests run on some of the spots in the trail of bloodstains on the stairs. If it was Marilyn's blood, he felt he could prove Sheppard had run this way with the dripping murder weapon. Of the stains tested, some were human bloodstains.

On July 13, three days after Sam was released from the hospital, the news about the other woman broke in a Cleveland paper. Louis B. Seltzer, editor of the *Cleveland Press*, wrote an editorial headlined THE FINGER OF SUSPICION. He spoke of the "tragic mishandling of the Sheppard murder investigation." He called for an end to "this nonsense of artificial politeness." He wanted someone to "smash" into this situation and "tear aside the curtain of hypocrisy" and solve the murder. There was, he wrote, "a husband who ought to have been subjected instantly to the same third degree to which any other person under similar circumstances is subjected" instead of being taken to his family's hospital.

Seltzer wrote editorial after editorial—one headline screamed SOMEONE IS GETTING AWAY WITH MURDER!—and they got a response. Metropolitan Cleveland police were called into the investigation to help the suburban force. Gerber rushed to call an inquest on July 21. On July 26 Susan Hayes, the other woman Sam Sheppard was accused of being involved with, was brought out from California.

Seltzer's *Press* kept pounding out demands that Sam Sheppard be arrested. He was "proved under oath to be a liar," but he was "still free to go about his business, shielded by his family, protected by a smart lawyer."

Authorities hesitated. They had little hard evidence against Sheppard. Why would he batter his wife to death? As a doctor, he'd know other murder methods. The night before she died, the two were affectionate and happy. If he had coolly staged that, could he have suddenly turned into a frenzied killer? If so, why? But on July 30, the police bowed to the *Press* and arrested Sheppard.

His trial began October 18 and lasted forty-three days. The official transcript contains more than two million words. An even larger number of words ran in the newspapers. About half the nation's newspapers reported the trial daily, giving it front-page coverage. The small Cleveland courtroom was crowded with more than fifty newspaper and radio-TV reporters. A managing editor for the Hearst papers said, "It's been a long time since there's been a murder trial this good." The Sheppard case had mystery, society, sex, and glamour. Newspapers would sell like hotcakes.

To keep the stories interesting, most reporters wrote what

people were eager to read, rather than reporting the facts presented in court. They asked why Koko, the family dog, hadn't barked that night. Surely the dog would bark at a stranger! Who else but Sam could have done it? A bushy-haired burglar? Not likely!

The prosecution claimed Sheppard's injuries were self-inflicted, and that his family had covered up for him in the hospital. Marilyn's bloodstained pillow was produced, along with Gerber's opinion about the mysterious surgical instrument. Brightly colored slides of the blood trail on the stairs were shown.

The defense countered with the testimony of an independent doctor, who said Sam Sheppard showed evidence of spinal damage. A dentist testified that Sheppard had two broken teeth. Both said he couldn't have inflicted these injuries on himself. The defense claimed that no one had ever seen the surgical instrument that could produce the imprint on the pillow and that no one ever would because it didn't exist.

After nearly a month, the "good for business" trial was boring. There simply wasn't much hard evidence. So reporters turned to reporting each other. Seltzer's *Press* was devoting two full columns a day to the trial, and one of their columnists, hard-pressed to write enough to fill those columns, reported a small courtroom drama:

Another reporter had had an attack of coughing and wheezing. One of Sam's brothers turned to the noisy reporter and said, "Drop dead." The reporter stopped coughing long enough to reply, "I can't. I've got to stay around for the hanging."

Harmless silliness? Perhaps, but it shows that the press had decided Sheppard was guilty before the jury said he was. The media had shaped public opinion when they cried for arrest.

Would they now cry for conviction? Would the jurors be able to judge the case on evidence? They could see the press's reaction in the courtroom.

The trial wore on and on until the press was frantic for something interesting to happen. Finally it did. The prosecution put its thirty-first and final witness on the stand, the other woman, Susan Hayes. She testified that she and Sam had been lovers. Sheppard, in rebutting this testimony *is reported* to have said, "What can I say?"

The public agreed solidly with the newspapers after they read about Hayes's testimony. Sheppard was a killer, and everyone knew why. But no one knew what the jury would decide when they withdrew.

What do *you* decide?

· VERDICT ·

Dr. Samuel Sheppard Found Guilty
of Second-Degree Murder, December 21, 1954;
Found Not Guilty, November 16, 1966

Dr. Samuel Sheppard before testifying to the grand jury.
(Wide World Photos)

The jury deliberated for five days, surrounded by 214 trial exhibits. They read passages from the trial transcript again and again, and they cast thirty ballots before they came to a conclusion. Sheppard was guilty of second-degree murder. He probably hadn't planned to kill his wife, but he had. Until the last day, two jurors voted not guilty.

On December 21, the night the verdict came in, Seltzer's *Press* sold thirty thousand more copies than usual. Seltzer said he was elated to have helped serve justice. Another editor, less concerned with circulation figures said, "the press will be answering its critics for years to come on what was done with this story."

Several days after the verdict, Sheppard's defense attorney finally obtained keys to the Sheppard house. He'd asked for them earlier and they had been denied. He hadn't insisted then, but now he did. If new evidence could be gathered, Sheppard could appeal.

Shortly after New Year's Day, an eminent criminologist from California, Dr. Paul Leland Kirk, arrived in Cleveland. He took photographs and measurements, then returned to California with his data. He built a scale-model bedroom and ran test after test on the shape and location of the blood spatters. Artificial plastic heads were battered with various weapons. What he found was startling.

A heavy flashlight had been used to kill Marilyn Sheppard. The blows had been delivered horizontally, not vertically. The bedroom door had been open at the time of the murder, the closet door had been closed. A "contact" spot on the closet door was different from the spatters made by drops flying from the murder weapon.

The killer stood beside or half-knelt on Marilyn's bed, intercepting the blood splatters that would otherwise have landed on the north and east walls. He or she would have been heavily blood-spattered. Sheppard's clothes were free of blood spattering. It wasn't likely that lying in the water would have washed them out completely. The blood spot on the knee of his wet trousers had been only partly dissolved by the wetness of the fabric, and it corresponded to a spot on the bed, precisely where he would have knelt to check his wife's pulse as he claimed.

The blood spatters on the walls also showed that the killer was either left-handed or ambidextrous (able to use either hand equally well). Sheppard was right-handed, period.

Marilyn's teeth had not been broken by the killer's blows as the prosecution said. Kirk's tests on dentures proved that only by pulling fingers or hands violently away could identical fragments be produced.

That led to an idea about the "contact" spot on the closet door. Had Marilyn bitten the killer's hand and drawn blood, and when he attempted to quiet her screaming, had the killer rested the bleeding hand on the closet door? It was impossible to discover the truth of this idea or gain any other information from the "contact" spot blood sample Kirk had taken to his laboratory. The sample was eight months old—too old.

The pillowcase, instead of being imprinted with the stain of a bloody surgical instrument, had probably been used either to smother Marilyn's cries or by Marilyn herself in an attempt to shield herself from the blows. Folding a blood-stained pillow produced the "mirror image" that looked like a double-pronged instrument.

The trail of spots on the stairs could not have been produced by blood dripping from a weapon. In Kirk's tests, the drops fell off any smooth weapon within a few yards. Furthermore, the prosecution had argued from a series of "bloodstains" that were perhaps not blood at all. Only some of the spots had been tested, and only some of those were human blood. Even if they *had* all been caused by Marilyn's blood dripping from a weapon, *any* murderer would have left them—not only Sam.

The defense immediately appealed. Their request was refused because, the judge said, they could have insisted they be allowed to investigate the house before the trial.

The defense appealed again on other grounds, always including prejudicial reporting. A convict confessed to the crime, but an appeal was denied. Lie detector tests taken by the convict and the Sheppard brothers and sisters-in-law, who were still suspected of a cover-up, resulted in a denied appeal. Appeal after appeal was rejected until a court finally ordered Sheppard's release in 1964—ten years after he was convicted.

But that ruling was overturned by another court in 1965. The judges said that even though the newspapers had greatly influenced Sheppard's trial, freeing him on those grounds would hurt the jury system:

"Our jury system cannot survive," said the judge, "if it is now proper to presume that jurors, selected with the care taken in this case, are without the intelligence, courage and integrity necessary to their obedience to the law's command that they ignore the kind of publicity here involved."

But finally on January 6, 1966, after hearing defense attorney F. Lee Bailey present the evidence in the case, the Supreme Court of the United States voted eight to one to overturn Sheppard's conviction. They ruled he hadn't had a fair trial because of "massive, pervasive, and prejudicial publicity." Sam Sheppard had won not freedom, but the right to a new trial.

It began on October 24, 1966—twelve years after the first. This jury heard Dr. Kirk's evidence. And this time, the press was controlled. On November 16, Sam Sheppard was found not guilty.

Sam Sheppard attempted to pick up his medical career but couldn't. He supported himself in a variety of ways, including "professional" wrestling. The press covered his life.

On April 6, 1970, he was found dead of natural causes in his home. The press covered his funeral.

Trial by Mob

I n 1927 Charles A. Lindbergh made the first solo, nonstop airplane flight from New York to Paris. Attempting only to win a $25,000 prize, he also won fame, an adoring public, and nicknames—"Lucky Lindy," the "Lone Eagle." He was a hero.

When his twenty-month-old son was kidnapped from the "farm" near Hopewell, New Jersey, at some time between 7:50 and 10:00 P.M. on March 1, 1932, people were outraged. The nation went on an emotional binge.

Sightings flooded in. Parents walking—even driving—with blond toddlers frequently were stopped, arrested, and detained until they could prove their child's identity. After they'd been stopped three times in one day, one couple in Upstate New York asked the police commissioner for a note saying their child was theirs!

Checking the reported sightings was one part of the local and state police's investigation. They'd been on the scene minutes after the kidnapping was discovered. In the nursery, the crib blankets still formed the outline of the missing toddler's body. Smudges of clay led from a window to the crib. An envelope lay on a radiator under the window. A state police fingerprint expert dusted the envelope and the note inside. The note said:

Dear Sir!
   Have 50.000$ redy 25.000$ in
20$ bills 15.000 in 10$ bills and
10.000$ in 5$ bills. After 2–4 days
we will inform you were to deliver
the Mony.
   We warn you for making anyding
public or for notify the Police
      the child is in gut care.
      Indication for all letters are
      singnature
      and 3 holes.

The "singnature" was a symbol: two quarter-sized, inter-locking circles drawn in blue ink with a solid red circle in the center, and three holes punched through the design.

It was too late to follow the kidnapper's instructions.

Outside the police found a crudely made, broken ladder about seventy feet from the nursery window. Police wondered if the homemade ladder was a plant, something put there to mislead them. It wasn't the right length to be convenient for kidnapping—the first rung reached only as high as thirty inches below the window.

Police reported finding only two footprints—one large and indistinct, as if a man had wrapped a towel around his shoe, and the other smaller, a woman's. They announced that one of the kidnappers was a woman, but retracted that when the small footprint was discovered to be Mrs. Lindbergh's.

They noted that the nursery window was scarred from being forced up. Finding a three-quarter-inch chisel in the mud below, police said the kidnapper had probably used that.

Strangely enough, the fingerprint expert reported finding no prints on the note or in the nursery. And the Lindberghs' dog had slept peacefully through the kidnapping, although it usually barked at even minor disturbances.

Police felt the most likely explanation was that a gang working with one or more of the family servants had taken the baby. The lack of fingerprints could mean that someone on the "inside" had wiped them away, and the timing of the kidnapping pointed to its being an inside job, too. If outsiders had stolen the child, they probably would have waited until the house was dark and everyone was sleeping.

Servants were questioned. Later one of them, threatened with being taken to the state police barracks for more questioning, committed suicide. Police announced this as an admission of guilt; she was a member of the kidnapping gang.

The press, who had learned of the kidnapping on the police teletype wire and streamed in with officials during the first, predawn hours of the investigation, snatched at each new bit of information. During the first week, most newspapers were filled with news of the Lindbergh tragedy.

At first Lindbergh welcomed the reporters. He and his wife wanted their child back, and he felt the police were more interested in finding the kidnappers than in the child's safety. Three days after their son was taken, the Lindberghs issued a statement urging the kidnappers to select a representative to meet one of theirs anytime, anyplace. They promised to keep arrangements confidential, and they promised no harm would come to the kidnappers. The statement cut the police out of ransom negotiations.

In fact, by this time the police were being cut out of much of the investigation. Several of Lindbergh's friends had set up a separate headquarters on the farm. The police were in the way, but they slogged on with work-a-day questioning in the neighborhood. Had anybody seen any suspicious strangers?

On March 5 the second note arrived, postmarked in Brooklyn. The ransom was higher now—$70,000. On March 6, a Dr. John F. Condon was reading about the case in his newspaper in the Bronx. Thoroughly incensed, he wrote a letter to the editor. He added $1,000 to the $25,000 reward already offered by the Lindberghs and said he'd be delighted to serve as intermediary between the family and the kidnappers. The newspaper ran his offer on the front page.

Three days later, Condon received an envelope. Inside was a note accepting his offer to serve as go-between. Also inside was a second, sealed envelope. Condon called Lindbergh, who until then was unaware of the man. Lindbergh told Condon to read the note over the phone. The letter gave instructions on delivering the ransom money. The symbol "singnature"—the pierced red and blue circles—appeared at the bottom. Because of the symbol, the Lindbergh group felt the letters were real. Although they weren't sure Condon was honest, they asked him to come to Hopewell for a conference. Condon did.

On March 12, back home in the Bronx, Condon received a phone call from someone with a German accent who claimed to be one of the kidnappers. Another person in the background had an Italian accent. Arrangements were made for a preliminary meeting at Woodlawn Cemetery.

When they met, Condon discovered the German-sounding man was a Scandinavian sailor named John. He said there were six members in the kidnap gang—four men and two women—and the baby was safe on a boat somewhere. "Cemetery John" promised to send the baby's sleeping suit as proof they actually had the child.

Lindbergh identified the sleeping suit when it arrived, and the ransom delivery plan went into action. The serial number of each bill was recorded as it was added to the pile. Some of the money was in gold notes, bills bearing gold seals. With the numbers and the additional signal of the gold seal, the kidnappers could be traced when they began passing the bills.

Lindbergh went with Condon to deliver the ransom at another cemetery, St. Raymond's. It was dark when they arrived. Condon and Lindbergh got out of the car. Condon said he wanted to talk to John alone first. As he walked off, leaving the money and Lindbergh behind, a voice called from the darkness: "Hey, Doctor!" Both Condon and Lindbergh heard the shout.

Condon turned and saw a man standing behind a tombstone. Drawing nearer, he recognized Cemetery John. John said the baby would be delivered six to eight hours after he got the money. Condon said he couldn't deliver the money until he got a receipt, a note telling where the baby was. John agreed, saying he'd go get one and be back in about ten minutes. After he left, Condon ran back to get the box of money. Thirteen minutes later, John handed over the note, Condon handed over the money, they shook hands, and Cemetery John vanished among the tombstones.

Condon took the note back to Lindbergh. The baby was on a boat—"boad" the note said—named Nelly in Buzzard's Bay, which separates Martha's Vineyard from the southern coast of Massachusetts.

The baby wasn't delivered. Hours later a search for the *Nelly* was mounted. It lasted two days. There was no such boat. Lindbergh followed other leads, searched for other boats. He was searching on the Atlantic on May 12, when a trucker left the road between Hopewell and Princeton and walked into the woods a short distance. He found the decomposed body of a child lying facedown.

Papers and radio stations immediately seized the news. LINDBERGH BABY FOUND DEAD! The child's nurse had identified fragments of clothes found beside the body. Lindbergh came to the morgue the next day. He looked at the remains for ninety seconds, counted the teeth, then said, "I am perfectly satisfied that that is my child." The body was cremated within the hour. No tests were done beyond a superficial autopsy.

The official report states that decomposition was so severe it wasn't even possible to determine the sex of the child. The left leg was missing from the knee down, the left hand and the right arm were missing, and so were all the major organs except the heart and liver. Death was caused by a fractured skull. There was also a small round hole on the right side of the skull, which the physician later said looked like a bullet hole.

Police weren't sure the body was the Lindbergh child. The child's body was too long to match the size recorded in young Lindbergh's medical records. Also, the "soft spot" on the head was too large for a child nearly two years old. And the body was unburied—simply covered with leaves—in an area that had been thoroughly searched. How could police, Boy Scouts, and local volunteers have overlooked it?

Police had other questions, too. Why was Condon so eager to get involved in the case? Was he an extortionist, taking advantage of the tragedy to make money? Was he working with Cemetery John as a member of the kidnapping gang? They tried to answer these questions while keeping a sharp eye on where the ransom money turned up.

The first bill appeared in Greenwich, Connecticut, passed

by a woman a week after the ransom was paid. One at a time, the bills trickled in in a circle around the Bronx. Some were passed by a man whose description seemed to match Cemetery John's. Those bills were oddly folded—in half lengthwise, then doubled over twice. But police efforts to catch those passing the bills failed.

A year after the kidnapping, President Franklin D. Roosevelt signed the Banking Relief Act ordering everyone who had gold currency valued at more than $100 to exchange it at banks for non-gold currency. Anyone hoarding gold would get a $10,000 fine or ten years in prison or both. Investigators were elated. The ransom money had included a large number of gold notes. Their recall could produce fresh leads.

Then, in the first weeks of 1934, the flow of folded ransom bills slowed to a stop. None appeared until September, when they suddenly turned up again. On September 18, a $10 gold note with a penciled note on the margin appeared: "4U-13-41, N.Y." A gas station attendant had jotted the license plate number of the man who'd given him the bill. He said the man had handed it to him, saying he had only about $100 of gold left.

Police rapidly traced the number to a man named Richard Bruno Hauptmann, who lived in the Bronx. Information on his license application showed he was thirty-four, blue-eyed, blond. Was Hauptmann Cemetery John? The application said he was a carpenter. Had he made the ladder? After twenty-eight months of coming up with nothing and being grilled in the press, police finally had a break!

The next day they watched as Hauptmann left his home and drove off. They followed him for fifty blocks, until he slowed behind a city sprinkler truck. The lead police car shot ahead and jolted to a stop in front of his car. Other police cars converged behind. An officer jumped into Hauptmann's car and pressed a gun against his chest.

Hauptmann showed no surprise. He pulled his car to the curb and opened the driver's door. Police dragged him out and snapped handcuffs on his wrists. Finally Hauptmann spoke. "What is this?" he asked in a thick German accent. Police recalled Condon's description of Cemetery John's "foreign" accent and smiled. This was it!

They found a $20 gold certificate with a ransom serial number in Hauptmann's wallet. The bill was unfolded. Where did he get it? the police demanded to know. How long had he had it? Did he have any more?

Hauptmann said he'd collected gold notes for two years. He'd seen paper money become worthless in his native Germany because of inflation, so every time he came across a gold certificate, he kept it. This was the last one he had.

Police reminded Hauptmann that he'd told the gas station attendant he had $100 of gold, and Hauptmann admitted he did. It was at home in a tin box. Police still hadn't mentioned the Lindbergh case; Hauptmann may have thought he was being held for illegally hoarding gold.

At Hauptmann's home, police didn't wait for a search warrant. When Hauptmann's wife, Anna, came in carrying the couple's infant son, Manfred, she was shocked. The place was ransacked—drawers pulled out and dumped, the mattress slashed. Police finally found the gold Hauptmann said he had—six gold coins.

It appeared police had come to a dead end once again. Then they thought of the garage behind the apartment house. They tore it apart . . . and found wads of ransom bills totaling $13,760 wrapped in newspapers!

Now Hauptmann was told he was under arrest for the Lindbergh kidnapping and taken to the police station, where he answered questions for hours and gave police handwriting samples. Hauptmann had alibis, but he also had a police record in Germany. Police suspected his alibis were lies. They called Condon in. He hedged when he identified Hauptmann as Cemetery John, but police were satisfied they'd found the kidnapper.

Official machinery ground into action. Hauptmann was indicted and his trial for the murder of Charles Lindbergh, Jr., set to begin January 2, 1935, in Flemington, New Jersey.

The press called it "the story of the century" and flooded to Flemington. There, the question was not whether Hauptmann was guilty. (Everyone assumed he was: A paper published by the Hearst syndicate ran a headline that said NATION ITSELF ACTS AS JURY TO TRY HAUPTMANN.) The big question was, how guilty was he? Would he die in the electric chair or serve a life sentence? That question was left up to the actual jury, eight men and four women—farmers, mechanics, and housewives—and they had a tough job.

Under New Jersey law, the jury in a capital case had to be sequestered (kept in seclusion, away from the reports and opinions in the news so they would respond only to evidence heard in court). But the jury for the Hauptmann trial was sequestered in the same hotel housing the reporters. They took their meals in the public dining room, separated by only a thin, cloth screen from journalists who shouted about "Hauptmann the baby-killer," the Nazi monster.

Furthermore, four times a day the jury moved from courthouse to hotel through reporters standing on the courthouse steps making bets on how long it would take to convict Hauptmann. On the street, people called to them: "Burn Hauptmann!" Souvenir sellers hustled reproductions of the kidnap ladder.

The Hearst papers assigned star trial reporter Adela Rogers

St. Johns to the case, and she produced headlines like KEEP YOUR HANDS OFF OUR CHILDREN. In 1931 there had been 279 kidnappings in the United States. The Lindbergh baby was the capper. Hearst even hired an attorney for Hauptmann in exchange for exclusive rights to all interviews with Mrs. Hauptmann. The Hauptmanns agreed to this because police had confiscated all their money and records.

The first thing the Hearst attorney did was order new stationery. The letterhead read: The Hauptmann-Lindbergh Trial/Edward J. Reilly/Chief Counsel. Running down the left-hand margin was a red drawing of the kidnap ladder. Reilly was free, but he was no bargain. The day before the trial opened, he was passed out from a lengthy New Year's Eve party. He didn't bother to discuss the case with Hauptmann, and he was openly contemptuous of the "hicks" on the jury.

State Attorney General David Wilentz led the prosecution. "We will prove to you beyond a reasonable doubt," he said, "that the man who committed this crime was Bruno Richard Hauptmann, and that it was Hauptmann alone." *Alone.* For the next thirteen days, Wilentz presented the major points in the prosecution's case:

• Eyewitnesses had seen Hauptmann near the farm. Lindbergh also identified Hauptmann on the basis of the words "Hey, Doctor!" he'd heard in the darkness outside St. Raymond's Cemetery as Condon went to meet Cemetery John.
• Handwriting experts gave their opinion that all the notes had been written by the same person—Hauptmann.
• Physical evidence of a board from Hauptmann's closet, on which Condon's phone number was written in what Hauptmann admitted looked like his handwriting, proved

that the man Condon met in the cemeteries was Hauptmann.

• Accountants testified that Hauptmann's stock-trading and bank accounts had grown after the ransom money was paid.

• Work records proved Hauptmann had quit his carpentry job on the day the ransom money was given to Cemetery John.

• Testimony proved the ransom money had been found in Hauptmann's garage.

• A wood expert testified that he traced the lumber used in making the ladder to Hauptmann.

• Evidence proved Hauptmann had taken a board from his own attic to make one of the side rails of the ladder—the famous Rail 16.

Hauptmann's chief counsel Reilly remained unconcerned. Usually Hauptmann spoke to C. Lloyd Fisher, a local lawyer. The defense's major arguments were these:

• Hauptmann's alibis were valid. He was with his wife on the kidnapping night, March 1, 1932. He had gone to pick her up from the bakery where she worked, as he did every Tuesday night. He had worked until 5:00 as a carpenter on April 2, 1932, the day Condon gave the ransom money to Cemetery John. He quit his job, went home, and a friend had come over at 7:00 as usual on the first Saturday of the month to talk and play music.

• Hauptmann's financial dealings were honest. On the stand, he explained them from memory, saying the police had taken his "big book"—a ledger. (Police denied there was such a book.) He said the large sums of money appearing in his accounts resulted from transferring funds almost daily to play the market.

• Eyewitnesses supported Hauptmann's explanation of why the ransom money was in his garage. Hauptmann claimed that a friend named Fisch, his partner in a fur- and stock-trading business, had given him the money in a shoe box for safekeeping in December 1933, before he went to Germany for a visit. The prosecution claimed this was a lie— a "Fisch story"—and, unfortunately, Fisch had died overseas. But defense witnesses said they'd seen Fisch give Hauptmann the shoe box. None of them had seen what was in the box. Neither had he, Hauptmann said, until he opened it in September 1934. He started spending the money inside because Fisch owed him money. He'd discovered Fisch was a crook, and he felt this was the best way to make sure he was repaid.

• When asked if he had made the crude ladder, Hauptmann said, "I am a carpenter." He meant only an unskilled amateur would turn out a crude piece of work like that. He asked why he would take a piece of wood from his attic for Rail 16 when his garage was full of wood and there was a lumberyard a block away.

His testimony was offered unemotionally in an accent so thick it was difficult to understand him.

The case went to the jury on the thirty-second day of the trial. Under New Jersey law, the judge can review evidence as well as instruct the jury on the law. Judge Trenchard's charge to the jury went over the prosecution's argument point by point: "The defendant says that the ransom money was left with him by one Fisch, a man now dead. Do *you* believe THAT?"

Over and over he asked, "Do *you* believe THAT?" and other questions such as "Is there any reason to doubt that prosecution witness?" And, "Is there any reason to believe the defendant?"

When the jury left to deliberate, they walked through excited crowds thronging the street. The jury was out for more than eleven hours, and for much of that time, the crowd chanted in the dark beneath their windows: "Kill Hauptmann! Kill Hauptmann! Kill Hauptmann!" When a man threw a rock at the courthouse and smashed a window, the mob moved to keep police from seizing him, still chanting: "Kill Hauptmann! Kill Hauptmann! Kill Hauptmann!"

What would you have said? Was Hauptmann guilty beyond a reasonable doubt? Should he have been executed? Should he have been let off easy with life in prison? Or should he have been found not guilty and freed?

· VERDICT ·

Richard Bruno Hauptmann
Found Guilty of Murder in the First Degree,
With No Recommendation for Mercy

Richard Bruno Hauptmann listening to his lawyer Edward J. Reilly
before taking the witness stand in his own behalf.

(Wide World Photos; National Archives)

The jury had voted Hauptmann guilty the moment they entered the jury room. The delay was caused by two members who wanted to recommend mercy.

After the verdict was in, Wilentz jumped up: "The state moves for immediate sentence." Somehow a man slipped from the locked courtroom and shouted to the street below from an open window: "Guilty—death!"

The mob went crazy, screaming and yelling and dancing for the newsreel cameras. Miles away, Lindbergh heard them over the radio. "That was a lynching crowd," he said. Earlier he'd told a dinner guest that Judge Trenchard's summation was biased.

Now even Judge Trenchard seemed surprised at the mob's behavior, but he pulled himself together quickly and asked the defendant to stand for sentencing. Hauptmann would be executed in the week beginning Monday, March 18, 1935.

Everyone "knew" Hauptmann was guilty, but not everyone believed it. His wife didn't. Perhaps that was to be expected. Defense lawyer Fisher didn't. Perhaps that was to be expected, too. Reilly, his chief counsel, didn't seem to care. Perhaps that was to be expected, too.

For reasons known only to himself, Reilly had thrown away chance after chance to help Hauptmann present his case. For example, he told two wood experts he didn't need their opinions to counter that of the state's expert. As a result the kidnap ladder was tied to Hauptmann. Reilly also never looked into the reports that police had beaten Hauptmann during questioning. He also ignored reports that Hauptmann had produced pages and pages of handwriting samples for police, while only some pages were produced in court. He accepted completely the identification of the dead baby found in the woods as young Charles Lindbergh.

What wasn't expected was New Jersey Governor Harold

Hoffman's reaction. According to Anthony Scaduto in *Scapegoat*, Hoffman didn't believe Hauptmann was guilty, and neither did some other eminent people. Charles Curtis, former Vice President of the United States, phoned Governor Hoffman to say he thought there were "a lot of funny things" about the case. Famous attorney Clarence Darrow sent Hoffman a telegram begging that Hauptmann's death sentence be commuted to life imprisonment. "No man should be executed on such flimsy evidence," Darrow wrote.

Hoffman worked with respected private investigators who had been on the case from the beginning and had traced the kidnapping to a man named Paul H. Wendel. According to Scaduto's book, Wendel confessed that he himself was Cemetery John and had taken the ransom money from Dr. Condon. The story goes that Wendel, a disbarred attorney, had once helped Isidor Fisch, his client, beat a drug rap. He turned to Fisch following President Roosevelt's call-in of gold notes to help sell some "hot" money. Since the numbers of the ransom bills were printed in the papers, Fisch immediately recognized them. Knowing he could easily keep the money since Wendel wouldn't report the theft to the police and wanting to take his planned trip to Germany, Fisch wrapped the money and gave it to his business partner Hauptmann for safekeeping. When Fisch died abroad, Hauptmann found and—innocently or stupidly—spent some of the money, with the results you know. On the advice of Prosecutor Wilentz—whose political ambitions would be stymied if Hauptmann, the defendant in the first criminal case he'd tried, were exonerated of the Lindbergh kidnapping—Wendel later retracted the confession and ultimately wrote articles and a book about the circumstances under which it had been given. Wendel thus became a junior-grade hero. The private investigators and their aides faced criminal charges. Wilentz continued to practice law, although he never became the political power he'd thought he might become.

As the time for the execution drew near, Hoffman gave Hauptmann a reprieve for seventy-two hours—all he could do under New Jersey law—and went into action to save Hauptmann's life. He asked the pardons board to commute the death sentence based on the strong evidence for Wendel's guilt and Hauptmann's innocence. He hoped a new grand jury would hear the evidence against Wendel and indict him. If they did, the pardons board couldn't let Hauptmann die. The plan failed, due in large part to Wilentz, whose responsibility as state attorney general it was to present the evidence against Wendel to the grand jury.

Somehow the completed paperwork charging Wendel with the murder of the Lindbergh baby never got to the grand jury. There was no official charge, so the grand jury had nothing to investigate. Obviously they couldn't indict Wendel.

Hauptmann was executed several nights later.

He still didn't understand what had happened to him; still softly declared in broken English his absolute innocence. But he made his peace with his God, said good-bye to his wife, looked at the pictures of his own small son one last time, courteously said thank you to the guards who unlocked the barred doors before him, and walked to the death chamber.

Could this story be true? Even an incomplete listing based on Scaduto's work of the suppressed or impeached evidence of eyewitnesses alone shows the prosecution—including attorneys and police—had worked too hard to convict Hauptmann. Of the eyewitnesses who told police they'd seen Hauptmann at Hopewell:

• one was partly blind, according to public-welfare records;

- one had identified so many men as the extortionist that Bronx police files bristled with his statements;
- one was a thief who had been dismissed from several jobs for stealing company funds, had just lost another job, and had described Hauptmann's car incorrectly;
- one admitted to Governor Hoffman that he'd lied under oath because he'd been promised part of the reward money.

Charles Lindbergh's voice identification of Hauptmann in the third day of the trial was certainly convincing to the jury. But he claimed to recognize Hauptmann's voice two years after hearing only two shouted words of a stranger. A witness's vocal identification is usually considered evidence only if the witness has had some familiarity with the person being identified.

Testimony from handwriting experts who disagreed with the prosecution's experts was suppressed. In fact, one penmanship expert came to Governor Hoffman after the trial to point out that Hauptmann wrote in the Palmer-Zaner penmanship style, whereas the ransom notes were written in the vertical round-hand style. He said if a person had been taught one penmanship style, it would be almost impossible to adopt another.

Other suppressions documented by Scaduto include the following:

- Police knew the window at the farm had been pried open by a screwdriver, not a chisel like the one they found below the window or those they confiscated from Hauptmann's tool box. Wendel was the only suspect who spoke of a screwdriver.
- Hauptmann's fingerprints weren't on any bills passed be-

fore September 1934, when he said he opened Fisch's shoe box and found the money.

• Police laboratory reports showed that under microscopic inspection bills passed by Hauptmann differed from bills passed earlier. They had been kept in different surroundings. The shoe box full of money wasn't a "Fisch story."

• Police records of *many* footprints found and gathered in the first hours of the investigation were kept secret. Police later confiscated all of Hauptmann's shoes.

• Letters from Fisch confirming Hauptmann's business relationship with him were confiscated by police, as were Hauptmann's ledger and money.

• Condon's phone number on the board from Hauptmann's closet was written by a reporter who then wrote a story about a new "clue." (Although this was common knowledge among the media, it was never printed or broadcast.)

Lies complicate any trial. The ones above were uncovered by a responsible journalist in public documents. They cast more than a reasonable doubt on Hauptmann's guilt.

But during Hauptmann's trial, most reporters ran with the mob. After his conviction, *Editor and Publisher*, a magazine for journalists, said:

"No trial in this century has so degraded the administration of justice. If the life of one man and the unhappiness of hundreds are to be commercialized for the benefit of entertainment, or radio broadcasters, newspaper publishers, newsreel producers; if a public trial . . . [does not mean] protection from the indignities of the mob, then the ancient institution of trial by a jury of peers is without meaning."

Before Hauptmann died, Governor Hoffman received a letter from a Midwestern judge. "Is it not much better that this man, who, after all, is an alien, should die," the judge wrote, "even if there were some doubt as to his guilt or innocence, than that there should be a reflection cast upon American courts?"

Prosecutor Wilentz described Hauptmann as a "master criminal." As a master criminal, Hauptmann made a better scapegoat.

Still missing is $31,140 of the ransom money. And even though all mention of a kidnap gang was avoided during the trial and Wendel went free, according to Scaduto, the New Jersey state police file on the Lindbergh case is still open. Officials still think others were involved.

How Many Jurors Are Enough?

A trial jury is usually made up of twelve jurors and a number of alternates. The alternates are chosen so that if a regular juror gets sick or must leave for some other reason, the trial can go on.

But there are extraordinary times when a new player enters the hockey game—the public itself, including the media. At such times, society can't wait for the jury to decide a criminal case on the basis of the evidence. The acceptance of biased or untruthful evidence is encouraged by the pressure for a verdict. The idea of innocent until proven guilty crumbles.

When the public, including the media, wants a scapegoat—someone who'll "get" it—the rules of evidence and judicial sanity can be swept away. The only thing that matters is "getting" the scapegoat. It happened in the Lindbergh kidnapping case when the mob demanded a victim, and in the Sheppard murder trial when the media wanted one.

Scapegoats can be groups as well as individuals. In Nazi Germany the scapegoats were the Jews, and in the desegregation struggles in the United States the scapegoats were the blacks.

The causes of this society-wide insanity have been carefully studied, and they're not especially flattering. Scapegoats are found to take the fall for society's fears, frustrations, guilts; to make people feel superior; to go along with the herd's actions and thoughts.

When a system of justice doesn't successfully resist the pressures of the public, it is worse than useless. When that failure leads to the execution of a person, it is *lawful* violence. That is a very dirty game, and it hurts us all—because the defendant isn't always someone else.

Society has lunatic times, and so, unfortunately, do individual members of society. What can a jury do when the accused in a crime is shockingly, breathtakingly insane? Decide the case on the basis of evidence, of course, as the juries did in the two astonishing cases that follow.

"A Clown Can
Get Away with Murder"

There was only a foot and a half of headroom in the crawlspace under the house. Police evidence technicians (ETs) drew back at the foul smell. They knew they couldn't work on hands and knees, so they sawed through the oak floor above before they began digging for the bodies John Wayne Gacy said he'd buried there.

Gacy hadn't lied. The bodies were packed foot to skull in shallow trenches. Police numbered them as they found them: No. 1. No. 3. (No. 2 was found in the meantime under a slab of concrete in the garage.) Names would come later—if dental records could be found that matched the teeth.

When ETs found the skull of No. 4 below the feet of No. 3, they wondered if there were *layers* of bodies. The idea was shocking, but not any more so than the rest of the case. They decided to dig under the gravesite of No. 1. They found another body beneath that one, too—No. 5. They dug on. No. 6. No. 7.

The ETs choked and dug on. Some of the bodies still had ropes around their necks. Gacy had spread lime down there for years, saying it cut the odor from stagnant water. The ETs wore surgical gloves to protect their hands from the stinging lime.

Nos. 19, 20, 21.

When scratched, an ET immediately got a tetanus shot to avoid infection. The men shaved at night so they wouldn't have fresh nicks on their faces when they were at the site.

No. 28.

That body, the last from the crawlspace, was found by the Friday after Christmas. Police began tearing apart the back-yard barbecue pit, suspecting more bodies would be found there. The weather turned bad, stopping that avenue of inves-tigation for a time.

But there was other evidence to gather. Police worked on, knowing they'd done the best possible job so far. The opera-tion had been photographed and videotaped; each skeleton had been tagged, placed in a bag, and carried off to be identi-fied in the laboratory. Work at the house on the northwest outskirts of Chicago in December 1978 had been done as carefully as a scientific excavation of an ancient Egyptian king's tomb.

In fact, the investigation of the crawlspace below 8213 Summerdale was much like an archeological dig . . . except that these bodies weren't ancient. The longest any of them had been there was six years. Most of them were the bodies of teenage boys.

The public wondered what had happened at 8213 Sum-merdale. If what police said was true, that small, yellow-brick ranch house was the lair of one of the worst mass murderers in history.

John Wayne Gacy didn't look notorious or insane. He was heavyset, a round-faced man with a double chin. At thirty-six, he owned a company called PDM (Painting, Decorating, and Maintenance) and many witnesses later testified that he was a "workhorse." His sister called him generous in easing family financial problems. Others, living victims, brokenly described him as something on the far side of evil.

To the Delta Unit of the Des Plaines police who had been called in to keep him under surveillance during the early investigation, Gacy was a pain. Keeping track of him was almost like a comedy film with a title like *The Mad, Mad, Mad World of the Surveillance of a Suspected Kidnapper.*

Kidnapping was all they suspected him of at the time. Fifteen-year-old Robert Piest had disappeared on December 21, 1978, after he finished work at a drugstore in Des Plaines. When his mother came to pick him up, he told her he had one more errand to run. "I've got to talk to a contractor about a summer job that will pay me five dollars an hour," he said before he walked outside. He wanted money to buy a car to impress a girl he was having troubles with. His mother understood. She waited.

When Rob didn't return, she drove home. It was her birthday, but the family waited to cut her cake until Rob came home. He didn't return that night. It wasn't like him; he was a star gymnast, a "straight" kid. The Piests filed a missing-persons report.

The suburban Des Plaines police force discovered who the contractor was and assigned the Delta Unit, an undercover drug-and-vice squad, to watch him, hoping he'd lead them to the boy. Gacy eluded them time and again, driving wildly on icy city streets and tearing down the freeway at one hundred MPH.

Delta Unit didn't have powerful cars or radios, but Gacy was helpful sometimes and told them where he was going. His attitude was mercurial. One minute he threatened a multi-thousand-dollar harassment suit, and the next minute he bought meals and drinks for the men tailing him. Once he invited them into his home for a fish dinner. The men from Delta Unit ate; Gacy picked at his food nervously.

Police knew that Gacy wasn't anxious because he didn't know how to cook. He'd once run three Kentucky Fried Chicken restaurants in Waterloo, Iowa. That was how he'd gotten his nickname of "Colonel" in the Waterloo Jaycees (the Junior Chamber of Commerce, a national organization of main-street-type businessmen). He'd managed pancake breakfasts for the Jaycees and had thrown parties for as many as four hundred friends, neighbors, and political leaders in Chicago.

Still, Gacy was nervous. He'd had run-ins with the police before. He'd been sentenced to ten years in Iowa's Men's Reformatory in Anamosa for attacking a teenage boy. His friends were astonished. "It was so hard for us to believe," said Charles Hill, a Waterloo motel manager. "He was such a good doggone Jaycee."

He was a good Jaycee in prison, too, where he served only twenty-one months of his ten-year sentence before he was paroled. During that time, he was a "model prisoner," a "power inmate." When he was released, a friend said, "Now that it's over with, keep your nose clean."

"I'll never go back to jail," Gacy said before he went to live in Chicago.

He avoided jail for a long time, despite parole violations and a Chicago Police Department rap sheet that includes FBI offenses. He'd learned what it took to make a charge stick.

Despite his legal history, Gacy was active in politics in Chicago, posing for photographs with the mayor and the First Lady of the United States. The head of his suburb's Democratic party organization said, "He was always available for any job: washing windows . . . playing clown for the kids at picnics and Christmas parties . . . I don't know anyone who didn't like him."

Dressed as Pogo the Clown, Gacy often entertained children in hospitals. When police first searched his home for anything that might prove Rob Piest had been there, they found a gallery of clown pictures in the living room. Later, surveillance teams would be astonished and alarmed when Gacy leaned over a restaurant table and confided, "A clown can get away with murder."

Police wondered if Gacy was saying he was a murderer. Or did he mean only that he could behave as outrageously as he wanted when he was Pogo, that a clown could say and do things an ordinary person couldn't?

As time went on, Gacy told them he was a murderer. But he said that another part of him—"Jack" or "John"—committed the murders. He was saying he was crazy, that he had another personality as Jack Hanley, a name he used when he cruised gay bars and dark streets.

Police weren't sure that proved Gacy was insane. They thought it probably proved only that Gacy knew how to use an alias. Gacy's former wife had called him a "police freak"; in Chicago he often told acquaintances to call City Hall and ask for Jack Hanley if they ever needed help. If any did, they found there really was an Officer James Hanley. If they didn't bother to check further, they didn't discover that Officer Hanley worked quietly in the hit-and-run unit north of the Loop.

To back up the suggestions he was a cop, Gacy drove a black Oldsmobile equipped with red spotlights. That, plus his PDM company (PD perhaps meaning police department?)

and his black leather, police-type jacket, terrified victims. By the time the investigation was finished, police knew how well Gacy's "police identity" worked. Thirty-three bodies had been found—in the crawlspace, in the garage, under the backyard barbecue, and in the Des Plaines River.

No. 33 seemed to be the last, but no one could be sure. Gacy had so many victims that he couldn't remember some of them. Some nights, he said, he "hit a double"—two killings. That troubled police because some of the recovered bodies couldn't be identified. But Gacy wasn't troubled. "They killed themselves," he claimed, but that turned out to be untrue as he demonstrated his "rope trick" during his confession to police.

It was a "killer clown's" trick. He looped a rope or a rosary around the neck, knotting it twice, then tightening it like a tourniquet with a stick. When his victims were dead, he buried most of them in the crawlspace.

But before he pulled the rope trick, Gacy calmly explained, he trapped his victims with a "handcuff trick." First he put handcuffs on himself and released them. Then he put handcuffs on the boys but refused to show them the unlocking trick. When they were helpless, he molested them.

There were only two reasons he killed, he said—if they "raised the price" or if they threatened him. Rob Piest angered Gacy by saying no and because Gacy thought he might tell. Gacy had another problem with Piest, his final victim. There was room to stuff the boy's blue parka under the floor of the utility room, but his crawlspace "burial grounds" was full. He dumped the body in the Des Plaines River.

People felt that Gacy must be insane, and Gacy agreed. In a Christmas Eve letter to his mother written after he'd been arrested, he said: "Please forgive me. . . . I have been very sick for a long time (both mentally and physically). . . . I wish I had had help sooner. May God forgive me."

On April 23, 1979, a Cook County grand jury indicted Gacy on thirty-three counts of murder. Two days later, Gacy was arraigned and he pleaded not guilty.

His trial began on February 6, 1980, before a jury of seven men and five women chosen from outside the city to avoid the effects of pretrial publicity. The question the jury would decide in Judge Garippo's courtroom was not if Gacy had committed the murders. He'd confessed to them, had demonstrated how he'd done them, and even had drawn a map of the crawlspace for police to follow in exhuming the bodies. As the defense put it, the jury's choice was simple: Either Gacy was evil or he was insane. Evidence presented over the next six weeks made it obvious the jury's choice wasn't so simple.

The prosecution called parents to testify about their murdered sons. An employee of PDM told of digging the burial trenches in the crawlspace at Gacy's orders, saying Gacy told him he wanted the trenches for drainage construction. The prosecution pointed out that this indicated that Gacy planned ahead to dispose of his victims. The implication was that he was in control of his actions and therefore sane. But a parade of experts would have more to say about Gacy's sanity.

The first expert for the defense said he thought Gacy was a person who looked normal on the surface but had all kinds of mental illnesses. He felt that Gacy was severely mentally ill—psychotic—but only at certain times. When Gacy was killing, he was temporarily insane and didn't know that what he was doing was wrong; later he became aware of it.

Further experts for the defense felt Gacy had mental problems, but they didn't agree on whether they thought he was insane when he killed. One was reluctant to give an opinion; another said he thought Gacy was aware that he was doing wrong when he murdered.

The first expert for the prosecution said Gacy was sane but antisocial, the kind of person often in conflict with society. That was a personality defect, not a psychosis, and it couldn't excuse Gacy's crimes. Another expert for the prosecution said he didn't think Gacy was psychotic; still another said he didn't believe anyone could have thirty-three cases of temporary insanity. And yet another said Gacy's life indicated he could think in a rational manner and thus he didn't meet the state's insanity-defense standard.

In fact, he added, Gacy was so sane that if the verdict were not guilty by reason of insanity and he were committed to a hospital for psychiatric treatment, he'd be free in a short time. "We find it very difficult to keep people in hospitals who in fact need to be there because of concern, which I can understand, that to hospitalize is a deprivation of civil rights."

The possibility that Gacy could ever be free in the streets again exploded in the newspapers, and Gacy asked the judge to declare a mistrial. He won the chance to speak in court, where he denied the importance of his confession, accused the press of taking everything out of context, and said police officers made self-serving statements. "I have been called every name under the sun in this courtroom, and half the time I leave not even knowing who I am." He said he was confused by the whole mess.

In the sixth week the trial drew to a close. In closing, the defense said Gacy wasn't all evil. He had done good. He was a Jekyll and Hyde, like the character in the Robert Louis Stevenson novel "He was so good and he was so bad, and the bad side of him is the personification of evil," the defense said. "Do you hold him responsible for that, or do you take the first step of having him studied to try to prevent something like this from happening again?" Don't decide on emotion, the defense lawyer told the jury. If we study Gacy, his victims won't have died in vain. The defense asked the jury to bring in a verdict of not guilty by reason of insanity.

The prosecution said there could be no room for sympathy. If anyone needed to study John Gacy, there would be plenty of time while appeals were going through. And if John Gacy were a Jekyll and Hyde character, the prosecution reminded the jury that in the novel Jekyll came to look forward to taking the potion that turned him into the evil Mr. Hyde; he grew to enjoy the power.

"Don't show sympathy!" the prosecutor repeated. He took the pictures of Gacy's victims from the display board one by one. "Show justice! Show the same sympathy and pity that *this* man showed when he took *these* lives and put them *there!*" He threw the pile of photographs into the trap door of the crawlspace that had been brought into court as evidence.

After the dramatic closing statements, Judge Garippo's charge to the jury was measured and calm. The verdict on each of the indictments had to be unanimous. There were only three possibilities—guilty, not guilty, or not guilty by reason of insanity. The jury deliberated in the locked courtroom among the displays of the evidence for two hours.

What do you think? Were John Wayne Gacy's mental problems so severe he couldn't be held responsible for his actions? Or was he simply evil?

· VERDICT ·

John Wayne Gacy
Found Guilty

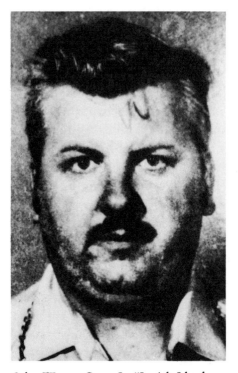

John Wayne Gacy, Jr. "I wish I had
had help sooner."
                    (Wide World Photos)

The jury found Gacy guilty on all counts, convicting him of more murders than anyone else in American history. Sentencing was set for March 13, 1980.

In March the prosecution requested a death sentence in

twelve of the cases because those murders had taken place since the new Illinois statute allowing capital punishment went into effect in 1977. The defense offered motions to declare the law unconstitutional. They said that the killings had begun before the death penalty went into effect and that the killings were a ritual series. Judge Garippo denied that motion and others.

Finally the defense chose to have the jury decide the sentence. The death sentence had to be unanimous. If only one person balked, the jury couldn't direct the court to deliver the death sentence.

Once again Judge Garippo instructed the jury. Once again they were out for two hours.

When they returned, John Gacy stood before the bench—in front of the judge—flanked by his two lawyers to hear the jury's decision:

"We, the jury, unanimously conclude that the court shall sentence the defendant, John Wayne Gacy, to death."

At the end of the sentencing, Judge Garippo thanked the jurors for their work, then went on speaking quietly: "A lot has been said about how much this case has cost, and I don't know what it cost. But whatever the cost was . . . it's a small price . . . that we paid for our freedom. What we do for the John Gacys, we'll do for everyone."

Gacy's execution has been postponed indefinitely until his appeals are resolved. On March 4, 1985, the Supreme Court of the United States refused to review the 1984 Illinois Supreme Court's decision to uphold the man's death sentence. Further appeals must—and probably will—be pursued again in state courts and, if necessary, lower federal courts if Gacy is to avoid execution.

Can a TV Camera Lie?

The cameraman stood in the mist outside the Hilton Hotel in Washington, D.C. Shortly before 2:30 P.M. on March 30, 1981, he rolled the video tape, recording President Ronald Reagan and his entourage as they left the hotel and walked to their limousines. In the next minute, the tape recorded something more chilling—a young gunman's arm and hand aiming at the President.

A voice yelled above the noise of the crowd. "President Reagan! President Reagan!"

The President turned toward the camera. The gunman crouched like a marksman and aimed. Six quick shots pocked the sound of city traffic.

The first shot pierced press secretary James Brady's head. The second struck police officer Thomas Delahanty in the back. The third went high, over the President's head and into the wall of a building across the street. The fourth caught Secret Service agent Timothy McCarthy in the chest. The fifth hit the bulletproof glass of the President's limousine. The sixth bounced from the end of the car into the President's chest, where it glanced off a rib and lodged in a lung, missing the heart by inches.

The tape ran on, recording Secret Service agents tackling

the gunman, John W. Hinckley, Jr. The agent later testified that Hinckley was still clicking his .22 as they fell, although he'd fired all the six exploding-head Devastator bullets he'd loaded into the weapon.

The tape was played and replayed by all three major television networks in the next several days until its impact had become almost—but not quite—routine.

After the shooting, police found a card in Hinckley's wallet. On it was printed the Second Amendment of the U.S. Constitution: "A well-regulated Militia, being necessary to the security of a free State, the right of the people to keep and bear arms, shall not be infringed." They also found several pictures of actress Jodie Foster.

In Hinckley's hotel room were clothes, bullets, a Band-Aid box with an airplane hijacking note folded in the bottom, a postcard with a picture of President and Mrs. Reagan on one side and a note to Jodie Foster on the other. The note said, in part, "One day you and I will occupy the White House and the peasants will drool with envy." There were paperback books, including *Taxi Driver*; pills, including Tylenol and Valium; and thirty-eight pages of Hinckley's own writings.

When Hinckley's trial began in May 1982, the cameraman's footage had made the whole nation eyewitnesses of his attempt to assassinate the President. But was he sane when he did it?

Pale, wearing a too-big tan suit and a loose brown tie, Hinckley looked younger than twenty-seven. He sat slump-shouldered facing the jury as the story of his life emerged from the testimony.

Born in Ardmore, Oklahoma, in 1955, he moved to Dallas with his family when he was four. In elementary school, John quarterbacked his football team, starred in basketball, was an avid Beatles fan. When he was in sixth grade, the family moved to a prominent Texas suburb. No longer a leader, John took to playing the guitar and managing the football team in junior high school. His mother said, "He had his own little withdrawn personality, and that was fine."

In 1973, after he graduated from high school, the family moved to Evergreen, Colorado, where his father established new headquarters for the family business, Vanderbilt Energy Corporation. John had no friends there, and he had none when he went back to Dallas to live with his sister and her husband. That fall he moved to his own apartment and began to dream of becoming famous as a musician or politician.

In the spring of 1975 he enrolled at Texas Tech at Lubbock, but dropped out the next spring and flew to California.

Six weeks later he wrote his parents that he'd found a "cozy, inexpensive apartment" and was trying to sell some songs he'd written. A month later, he wrote that someone had broken into his apartment and stolen everything. He'd been without food or clothing for two and a half weeks. He asked for money; his parents sent it.

Throughout the summer he looked for work and found none. He tried to make contacts in the music business and couldn't, although in August he wrote to tell his parents he was anticipating cutting a demo, or demonstration recording, to be used in auditioning for vocal work. He said he'd met a girl named Lynn Collins and they were friends. In fact, there was no such girlfriend, and there was little chance of his cutting the demo.

In September he wrote that he was tired of "the entire weird, phony, impersonal Hollywood scene" and was coming home. He didn't mention he'd seen a film called *Taxi Driver*.

Back in Evergreen, he worked as a busboy in a local supper club through the early winter. "I was self-supporting for the first and only period in my life. I was 21 years old," he wrote in an autobiography for Dr. John Hopper, the Colorado psychiatrist whom he saw from October 1980 through February 1981.

He left that job to return to Lubbock in March. There, he experienced a series of minor ailments and became enchanted with the politics of the American Nazis. He moved often and grew interested in guns. By the time he was twenty-four, he had founded the American Front. He called it "the Party for the proud White conservative who would rather wear coats and ties instead of swastikas and sheets." He named himself National Director of the American Front and created the whole organization, including a list of members from thirty-seven states. None of them existed.

Several addresses and ailments later, he formed a mail-order company called Listalot, which sold lists of names of customers who responded to ads in national magazines. The company was real; the names were not. Illnesses, many of them anxiety-related, continued to plague him, and his interest in firearms grew.

In May 1980, he read in *People* magazine that Jodie Foster, a star of *Taxi Driver*, planned to attend Yale. In September he talked his parents into letting him sell 350 shares of Vanderbilt Energy stock to pay for a writing course at Yale. He went to New York, registered at the costly Sheraton Park Plaza, and wrote his sister and brother-in-law that he didn't like Yale much because the students dressed like slobs.

He phoned Jodie Foster on September 20 and taped their conversation; the tape was later played at his trial. He called her again on the twenty-second before he flew back to Colorado. On September 24, he flew to Lubbock, Texas, and, with the money from the sale of his stocks, bought two handguns and travelers' checks. On September 27 he flew to Washington, D.C.; on September 28, to Columbus, Ohio; on September 30, he took a bus to Dayton. President Jimmy Carter was due to visit that city and Hinckley had his weapons ready, but he decided on October 2 not to kill Carter.

Instead he put his guns in a locker and left for New Haven and Yale University. He stayed there three days, sending unanswered notes to Jodie Foster.

The days that followed were filled with more frantic travel to other cities, further decisions not to assassinate President Carter, an arrest for attempting to carry firearms aboard an airplane. He returned home, overdosed on an antidepressant drug, and started seeing psychiatrist Hopper at his parents' insistence.

When former Beatle John Lennon was shot on December 8, he took a train to New York and joined the vigil in Central Park. By February 1981, he had been to New Haven eight times, each time attempting to contact Jodie Foster. By March 5, 1981, he'd traveled so far so fast that he'd run out of money.

His father sent him money to fly home, met him at the airport, and gave him $210 before he sent him back out on his own. John stayed in motels, selling some guns he'd bought by this time and other personal possessions, until March 25, when his mother drove him to the airport and gave him more money to see him on his way.

He flew to Hollywood, staying only a day before he realized again that he wouldn't find success there. He took a bus from Los Angeles to Washington, through Cleveland and Pittsburgh.

On March 30 he woke, took some Valium, got breakfast at McDonald's, came back to his room. When he couldn't nap, he read the *Washington Star* he'd bought after breakfast. It contained the President's schedule.

It was now almost noon.

He showered, took more Valium to calm down, loaded his .22 with Devastator bullets, and wrote to Jodie Foster:

> There is a definite possibility that I will be killed in my attempt to get Reagan. . . . I will admit to you that the reason I'm going ahead with this attempt now is because I just cannot wait any longer to impress you. . . . This letter is being written only an hour before I leave for the Hilton Hotel. Jodie, I'm asking you to please look into your heart and at least give me the chance, with this historical deed, to gain your respect and love.

At about 1:30, John put on a jacket and left for the Hilton. In one pocket was a red John Lennon button; in the other was his loaded .22. He saw the President enter the hotel. The President waved at the crowd gathered outside; Hinckley waved back. A short time later the President came out. It was 2:25 P.M. Hinckley waited until he was in firing range, then quickly squeezed off the six bullets.

During the trial, firearms experts, members of Hinckley's family, Jodie Foster on video tape, and others testified. But the real issue was Hinckley's sanity. Because three of the thirteen counts against Hinckley were federal, the provisions of the District of Columbia's insanity law had to be met. That meant that psychiatrists had to find that Hinckley suffered from a mental abnormality, then the jury had to find that

Hinckley couldn't tell right from wrong because of that abnormality.

The defense's first expert witness said Hinckley had a major depressive disorder and process schizophrenia. When a person thinks normal events like Jodie Foster's appearance in a movie is happening just for him, that person is suffering from process schizophrenia. He said Hinckley couldn't be held responsible for his actions.

The second expert witness for the defense saw Hinckley as being at the mercy of the books he read and the movies he saw. He said Hinckley had stolen the behavior of the character Travis Bickle, who throughout the movie *Taxi Driver* prepared to assassinate a politician running for office. He had stolen the words he used in the hijacking note he'd left in his hotel room in the bottom of a Band-Aid box from a novel. Hinckley couldn't plan well enough to pretend the symptoms of insanity discovered during this expert's interviews with him. The doctor said CAT scans (photographs of the brain) had shown patterns in Hinckley's brain common to many schizophrenics.

Another expert witness for the defense said Hinckley had scored 113—"bright normal"—on an adult intelligence test. But on the most commonly used test in forensic (or legal) psychology, Hinckley's score was exceptionally high, which wasn't good. It meant that the chance that he *didn't* have serious mental problems was one in a million.

The final expert witness for the defense wasn't helpful to them. He found himself admitting to the prosecution that Hinckley had lied when he said he'd selected the bullets used in the shooting randomly, without plan.

The prosecution's first expert witness was the forensic psychiatrist who'd led the government's team of experts in preparing a 628-page report on Hinckley's sanity. He said

Hinckley was suffering from a depressive neurosis and three personality disorders, but he wasn't as sick as the defense would have the jury believe. Instead, John Hinckley was lazy. He was self-centered, out after easy fame, a pampered loner who tricked his parents out of money.

This doctor said Hinckley had spent the year before the shooting choosing among several "high-publicity crimes" to impress Jodie Foster. He said Hinckley saw the assassination attempt as successful because he finally got Foster's attention. He knew attempting to kill the President was wrong.

The prosecution's second and final expert was the court-appointed doctor who had spent more time with Hinckley than any other psychiatrist. She said Hinckley's personality disorders weren't normal, but they didn't stop him from being responsible for his actions. She didn't believe Hinckley shot at the President to win Jodie Foster's love. (Hinckley shouted, "You're wrong!") She said Hinckley told her that just before he pulled the trigger, he thought he'd never have a better opportunity.

The jury saw the CAT scans and *Taxi Driver*, and the two-month trial wound down. Closing arguments summed up the testimony.

The prosecution asked if Hinckley was out of control, how could he hit four people with six shots? The prosecutor pointed out that Hinckley's insanity defense boiled down to four types of schizophrenia, Valium, *Taxi Driver*, Jodie Foster, CAT scans, John Lennon—"so many claims, he really doesn't have any at all." Hinckley had had fine parents and psychiatric help, and the reason he was pleading insanity was that he didn't want to take the responsibility for anything, including something as serious as an assassination attempt on the President of the United States!

The prosecution went on. Only hours before he made that

attempt, Hinckley wrote to Jodie Foster that he planned to "get" the President. While he stood outside the Hilton, he thought about killing, and with the gun in his hand he thought, I'll never have a better opportunity. Hinckley, said the prosecution, was not insane. He wasn't normal, but he knew what he was doing. He was responsible for his acts.

The defense said the opinions of the prosecution's experts were perhaps not the best. One had had only two years of forensic experience before interviewing Hinckley; the other had had only four.

The defense, not relying on the opinions of doctors, had also produced evidence from Hinckley's family and his own rambling writings. All their evidence showed "the gradual deterioration of the human mind over a period of many years" from high school on. John Hinckley had had no friends; he knew the world only from fast-food restaurants, supermarkets, and airports. He set himself impossible goals in an attempt to be a part of a successful family. He considered murder to be his only means of winning a girlfriend.

"It's pathetic," the defense said, "but it's delusional." Hinckley lived in an unreal world. He had no idea what he was doing. He couldn't be held responsible for his acts.

Hinckley slumped, his face pale. As he listened to his defense attorney call him pathetic, his mouth quivered and he cried quietly.

The judge gave the jury two key instructions. The first was that the prosecution had the burden of proof. The government had to prove beyond a reasonable doubt that Hinckley wasn't insane at the time of the shooting, or that he could have stopped himself. The second key instruction was that if the jury returned with a verdict of not guilty by reason of insanity, it was the court's duty to commit Hinckley to a mental hospital. He would remain there until the court found that most evidence indicated he wasn't likely to hurt himself or others.

The jury went into deliberation. They hadn't been allowed to take notes, and now they asked the judge for information. Some requests were honored (a list of evidence) and some were declined (transcripts of the parents' testimony, an expert's testimony about Hinckley's early years, a dictionary to look up the definitions of *poetry* and *fiction*). By Monday evening at 6:20 they'd reached a verdict.

Would you have said John Hinckley, Jr., was guilty or not guilty by reason of insanity?

· VERDICT ·

John Hinckley, Jr.,
Found Not Guilty by Reason of Insanity

John Hinckley, Jr., at the time of his high school grad-
uation, before what his defense called the "gradual
deterioration" of his mind began.

(Wide World Photos)

The judge silently flipped through the verdict given him by the foreman of the jury, then read: "As to count one, not guilty by reason of insanity." The verdict was the same for the remaining twelve counts.

Hinckley rocked on his heels and nodded his head, but the verdict was a surprise. He'd expected to be convicted, had even written a speech to read about it.

The judge remanded Hinckley to St. Elizabeths, a mental hospital. The sentencing session lasted eight minutes, but the aftermath of the trial proved to be more long-lasting.

One of the immediate effects was that the cost of the trial was toted up—$2.5 to $3 million. The attitude was sharply different from Judge Garippo's in the Gacy case, when he said that whatever the cost "it's a small price . . . that we paid for our freedom."

Another immediate effect was that the jurors in the Hinckley case were themselves questioned. Why did they acquit? Why not "guilty but insane," someone asked one of them. The juror replied, "We weren't lawmakers. We had to give a judgment back the way it was given to us. The evidence being what it was, we were required to send John back insane."

The questions kept coming at the jurors. A couple of them said they'd been pressured into acquitting Hinckley. Some appeared before the Senate Subcommittee on Criminal Law, and a few senators later said they thought the jurors hadn't understood the judge's instructions. Another juror, smarting at the accusations that the jury had focused on Hinckley's mental problems rather than on his criminal responsibility, said that she and the other jurors had understood their job.

A defendant who has been found not guilty by reason of insanity must be released from the hospital if he can prove he's no longer dangerous to himself or others because of his mental illness. Federal law gives people committed to mental hospitals the right to petition for their release every six months. In July 1984 John Hinckley petitioned for release for the first time. It was denied.

President Reagan, in a 1983 interview, said, "I just think it would be fine if he could be cured." By March 1984, he had sent Congress legislation that would abolish the plea of not guilty by reason of insanity.

The Line Between Insanity and Guilt

What behavior is insane? What behavior is guilty? There are guidelines to help a jury decide, but the guidelines—like so much of the law—keep changing.

Since biblical times, people who had no idea what they were doing when they committed a crime have been considered to be somehow outside the law. Most people who *did* know what they were doing felt the insane couldn't be punished if they killed someone, thinking they were eliminating a vicious tree. Such people weren't responsible for their actions; they weren't morally guilty. Still, there was always an uneasiness because legally such persons *were* guilty. What was society to do with them?

The formal ruling that gave moral hesitance a legal basis in American law happened in England in 1843. A man named Daniel M'Naghten thought he was being persecuted by the Pope, the Jesuits, and Prime Minister Peel. He decided to do something about it and went out to gun down Peel. Instead, he shot Peel's secretary. When he was found not guilty by reason of insanity, the British government wondered if the verdict would encourage crime.

Parliament asked Lord Chief Justice Tindal to look at the problem, and Tindal wrote what became the M'Naghten rule, which established a "right-wrong" test for the insanity defense. A person is not responsible for his criminal actions when he doesn't know what he does is wrong.

135

In 1881 the insanity defense was used unsuccessfully in the District of Columbia in behalf of Charles Guiteau, who killed President James Garfield. During his two-month trial, Guiteau read newspapers, occasionally shouting his contempt for the "poodle dogs in the newspaper business."

His defense explained that his "insane delusion" was that God had instructed him "to remove the President for the good of the American people." Guiteau claimed he didn't have any free will because he "had to do it." He was convicted and hanged. Because he knew his action was wrong even though he felt compelled to it, his case established M'Naghten as the rule of law in the District of Columbia.

The M'Naghten "right-wrong" rule held there until 1943, when the Durham rule added another facet to it. The Durham rule suggested that persons could know right from wrong, but maybe they didn't *feel* a criminal act was wrong or couldn't stop themselves from doing it. A person who would be convicted under the M'Naghten rule could be acquitted under the Durham rule.

In the next ten years, local Washington, D.C., courts became a testing ground for the insanity defense. In 1972, the Brawner rule refined the Durham rule, expanding the legal notion of not being able to stop oneself, or "irresistible impulse," as a test for the insanity defense.

The grounds for using the insanity defense in the United States were expanding. So were crime rates. The FBI's 1982 Index of Crime said the number of U. S. crimes since 1960 was up 400 percent. Violent crimes had increased sharply. People had started to think crime was completely out of control; they felt it was time to enforce the law and began to look more skeptically at what they saw as the overuse of the insanity defense. The Hinckley trial crystallized society's thinking.

Within a month after the verdict, committees of the House and Senate held hearings on the insanity defense. Attorney General William French Smith spoke for the Reagan administration in support of a new test to be applied by juries judging the defense. He told the Senate Judiciary Committee that "the criminal justice system has tilted too decidedly in favor of the rights of criminals and against the rights of society." Attorney General Smith expressed concern that psychiatrists were taking over some of the jury's function, that expert opinions were confusing, inconclusive, and incompetent in a court of law. Some prominent psychiatrists agreed, and so did a large portion of the public. Society—people—looked at the Hinckley verdict and asked if the courts were too permissive. Was that why moral values were falling all over the nation? Why crime rates were skyrocketing?

The new test suggested by Smith was called *mens rea*—"guilty mind." If an accused person meant to commit a crime, he could be convicted even if he was motivated by lunatic reasons. The *mens rea* test in the Reagan-supported federal legislation would shift the burden of proof in insanity cases. The prosecution would no longer have to prove a defendant sane; the defense would have to prove he was crazy. The alternate verdict of "guilty but mentally ill," which the jurors in the Hinckley case had been questioned about, wouldn't be possible, and the idea of "irresistible impulse" would be dropped. The proposed federal legislation would be the first national law about the insanity defense. It returned to the "right-wrong" test of the M'Naghten rule, which sixteen states still used, and elaborated on it by allowing conviction if the insane person was deemed aware of his intentions.

But will a federal law fix what society sees as abuse of the insanity defense in violent crimes?

Before Hinckley's trial, an Associated Press–NBC poll

found that 87 percent of a public sampling believed too many murderers were using the insanity plea to avoid jail. But in fact, most persons acquitted due to insanity are not murderers, assassins, or rapists. Outside New York and Michigan, the insanity defense is used mostly in nonviolent crimes like forgery, shoplifting, and car theft. Also, most insanity cases are settled out of court by attorneys or tried before judges only. Insanity defenses don't usually mean confusing a jury with conflicting expert testimony.

Still, much of society seems to support the "right-wrong" *mens rea* test. People say it will reduce the number of insanity acquittals. But what was an insanity case before may now become a diminished-capacity case. In diminished-capacity, the defendant can be convicted of a lesser crime than, say, murder.

In November 1983, the American Medical Association called for an end to the insanity defense. The American Bar Association and the American Psychiatric Association both think the defense should be kept. This is only a small part of the controversy over the defense; the Hinckley trial has resulted in firm support for the rights of society over the rights of the individual.

Within two years after the verdict, for example, half the states legally restricted the use of the insanity defense. The U.S. Senate voted ninety-one to one to support the administration's wish to return to the M'Naghten rule, saying their choice was between the forces of law and the forces of lawlessness. The House of Representatives voted against it.

Does the insanity defense give criminal law a moral basis? Or do criminals use the insanity defense to escape the law?

As a member of society, you're the jury . . . and the verdict is still out.

Summation

You've seen how guilt or lack of guilt can be decided without a jury, and you've seen how juries can fail—because of blind spots in their own thinking or because of blind spots imposed by the media or the mob. Yet in the United States, juries must decide cases of life and death on the basis of the body of evidence. Sometimes that evidence is grisly, unpleasant, insane. Even so, it's the jury's job to listen and decide.

The cases in this book were chosen because of their fame. Famous cases become that way because they are controversial and sufficiently interesting that people talk about them, sometimes questioning the way they were handled by the legal system.

That's good. If any system is questioned, it's an indication that it's alive and responsive, capable of changing to meet the demands of a new reality, of evolving to reach the goal of justice for all.

Our society's goal of justice for all is, however, unreached. Perhaps it's unreachable. After all, we are human and therefore flawed; our laws and our applications of them reflect those individual flaws.

But in many cases—perhaps most—our laws work well,

which is reassuring, if not particularly interesting. It is the occasional "squeaky-wheel case" that needs—and gets—attention in order to move toward the goal.

These squeaky-wheel cases and the questions that arose from them are an indication that the spirit of justice continues to thrive.

Bibliography

Abraham, Henry J. *The Judicial Process.* 2d ed. New York: Oxford University Press, 1968.

Abrahamsen, David. *The Mind of the Accused.* New York: Simon & Schuster, 1983.

Allport, Gordon W. *The ABC's of Scapegoating.* Freedom Pamphlets of the Anti-Defamation League of B'nai B'rith.

Aymar, Brandt, and Edward Sagarin. *Laws and Trials That Created History.* New York: Crown Publishers, 1974.

Bailey, F. Lee (with Harvey Aronson). *The Defense Never Rests.* New York: Stein and Day, 1971.

Brindze, Ruth. *All About Courts and the Law.* New York: Random House (Juvenile), 1964.

Caplan, Lincoln. "Annals of Law (The Insanity Defense)." *The New Yorker,* July 2, 1984: 45–78.

Ehrmann, Herbert B. *The Case That Will Not Die: Commonwealth v. Sacco and Vanzetti.* Boston: Little, Brown, 1969.

Englebardt, Leland S. *You Have a Right: A Guide for Minors.* New York: Lothrop, Lee & Shepard (Juvenile), 1979.

Fincher, E. B. *The American Legal System.* New York: Franklin Watts (Juvenile), 1980.

Frankfurter, Felix. *The Case of Sacco and Vanzetti: A Critical Analysis for Lawyers and Laymen.* Boston: Little, Brown, 1927.

Gaute, J. H. H., and Robin Odell. *Murder "Whatdunit."* New York: St. Martin's Press, 1982.

Gross, Gerald, ed. *Masterpieces of Murder: An Edmund Pearson True Crime Reader.* Boston: Little, Brown, 1963.

Klotter, John C., and Carl L. Meier. *Criminal Evidence for Police.* 2d ed. Cincinnati: W. H. Anderson, 1975.

Lincoln, Victoria. *A Private Disgrace: Lizzie Borden by Daylight.* New York: G. P. Putnam's Sons, 1967.

Menninger, Dr. Karl. *The Crime of Punishment.* New York: The Viking Press, 1968.

Pearson, Edmund Lester. *Studies in Murder.* Garden City, N.Y.: Garden City Publishing Company, 1924.

Pollack, Sir Frederick. "The King's Peace in the Middle Ages," in *Select Essays in Anglo-American Legal History*: 403–17. Boston: Little, Brown, 1908.

Read, Piers Paul. *Alive.* New York: J. B. Lippincott, 1974; Avon Books, 1975.

Scaduto, Anthony. *Scapegoat: The Lonesome Death of Bruno Richard Hauptmann.* New York: G. P. Putnam's Sons, 1976.

Simpson, A. W. Brian. *Cannibalism and the Common Law.* Chicago: University of Chicago Press, 1984.

Snow, Edward Rowe. *Piracy, Mutiny and Murder.* New York: Dodd, Mead, 1959.

Spiering, Frank. *Lizzie.* New York: Random House, 1984.

Stephen, Sir James Fitzjames. "Criminal Procedure from the Thirteenth to the Eighteenth Century," in *Select Essays in Anglo-American Legal History*: 443–530. Boston: Little, Brown, 1908.

Sullivan, Terry, and Peter T. Maiken. *Killer Clown.* New York: Grosset & Dunlap, 1983; Pinnacle Books, 1984.

Swiger, Elinor Porter. *The Law and You: A Handbook for Young People.* New York: Bobbs-Merrill (Juvenile), 1973.

Thayer, James Bradley. "The Older Modes of Trial," in *Select Essays in Anglo-American Legal History*: 367–402. Boston: Little, Brown, 1908.

Thorwald, Jurgen. *Crime and Science: The New Frontier in Criminology.* 1966. Reprint. New York: Harcourt, Brace & World, 1967.

Weeks, Robert P., ed. *Commonwealth vs. Sacco and Vanzetti.* Englewood Cliffs, N.J.: Prentice-Hall, 1958.

Wigmore, John Henry. "A General Survey of the History of the Rules of Evidence," in *Select Essays in Anglo-American Legal History*: 691–701. Boston: Little, Brown, 1908.

Index

Accused (the), 3–4, 52, 54, 74
Acquittal, 33, 54, 138
Aliens, radical, 42–43
  see also Foreignness
American Bar Association, 138
American Front, 125
American Legal System, The
  (Fincher), 55
American Medical Association,
  138
American Psychiatric Associa-
  tion, 138
Anderson, George W., 43, 48
Anderson, Maxwell, 48
Anderson, Sherwood, 48
Andes survivors, 12–20, 22–
  23, 24
Andrews, Lola, 45, 49
Appeal(s), 48, 49, 52, 54, 64,
  87–88, 121
Arraignment, 33
Associated Press-NBC poll
  about insanity defense,
  137–38

Bailey, F. Lee, 87
Banking Relief Act, 95
Beane, Sawney, Family, 5–11,
  21, 22, 24
Blacks, 109

Blaisdell (judge in Lizzie Borden
  case), 33
Boda (car owner in Sacco-
  Vanzetti case), 43, 45, 46
Borden, Abby, 26, 27, 28, 29,
  30, 31, 32
Borden, Andrew, 26, 27, 28, 29,
  30, 31, 32, 38
Borden, Emma, 27, 28, 30, 31,
  32, 34, 38, 39
Borden, Lizzie, 26–39, 53, 54–
  55
  confession, 38
Bowen, Dr., 29, 30
Bowen, James, 122
Brawner rule (insanity defense),
  136
Briggs (governor of Massachu-
  setts), 64
Burden of proof, 52
  in insanity cases, 137

Cambodia, 23
Canessa, Roberto, 12–14, 16, 17
Cannibalism, 5–11, 12–20,
  21–23
  psychological effect of, on
  survivors, 17–18, 20, 23
Carter, Jimmy, 126
CAT scans, 128, 129

"Cemetery John," 92, 93, 95, 96, 97, 98, 99, 104
Churchill, Adelaide, 29–30
Circumstantial evidence, 62–63, 68, 75–76
Cleveland Press, 80–81, 82, 85
Communists in U.S., 42–43
Condon, John F., 92–93, 94, 96, 97, 98–99, 104, 107
Confession(s), 49, 54, 64–65, 87, 104, 117, 118
Constitutional rights, 41, 42–43, 74
see also Criminals, rights of
Conviction, 3, 33
Corroborating evidence, 74
Courts, criminal, 3–4
Crime rates (U.S.), 136, 137
see also Violent crime(s)
Criminal justice system, 3–4, 52, 109–10, 137
Criminal offenses, 23
Criminal record(s), 74
Criminals, rights of, 137
Cross-examination, 74
Cumulative evidence, 74
Curtis, Charles, 104

Darrow, Clarence, 104
Death penalty, 3, 34, 35, 49–50, 103–8, 120–21
Defendant(s), 110
see also Accused (the)
Defense, 3, 52
    Gacy case, 117–19, 121
    Hinckley case, 128, 130
    in insanity cases, 137
    Lindbergh case, 99–100
    Lizzie Borden case, 34–36, 38, 53

necessity as, 21–22
Parkman case, 62–63
Sacco-Vanzetti case, 44–45, 49
Sheppard case, 82, 85, 86
and suppression of evidence, 52–53
Wallace case, 69–70
Delahanty, Thomas, 122
Delgado, Alfredo, 19
Desegregation, 109
Des Plaines (Ill.) police, Delta Unit, 113–14
Diminished-capacity case(s), 138
Direct evidence, 74–75
Documentary evidence, 74
Dos Passos, John, 48
Double jeopardy, 54
Dreyfus, Alfred, 48
Durham rule (insanity defense), 136

Editor and Publisher (magazine), 107
Ehrmann, Herbert B., 49
Einstein, Albert, 48
England, 25
    law, 24, 53
Evidence, 3, 4, 33, 52, 55
    body of, 73–76, 139
    cannibalism case, Uruguayan rugby team, 14, 16
    Gacy case, 111–12
    inadmissible, 73–74
    kinds of, 74–75
    Lindbergh case, 89–91, 98–99, 103, 104, 105–7
    Lizzie Borden case, 28, 29, 30, 34, 35, 39

Evidence (*cont'd*)
  new, 54, 85–87
  Parkman case, 61, 62–63, 75
  in Roman law, 54
  rules of, 73–74, 109
  Sacco-Vanzetti case, 44, 45–
    46, 48
  Sheppard case, 78, 79, 80, 81,
    82, 85–87
  suppression of, 49, 52–53,
    105–7
  Wallace case, 66–67, 69, 71,
    72
Evidence technicians (ETs):
  Gacy case, 111–12
Executions, 105, 110, 121
Expert testimony, 52, 74, 137,
    138
  Gacy case, 117–18
  Hinckley trial, 127–30, 131
  Lindbergh case, 98, 99, 103,
    106
  Sacco-Vanzetti case, 44, 45,
    49
Eyewitness(es), 74–75, 76
  Lindbergh case, 98, 100,
    105–6
  Parkman case, 59–60, 63
  television as, 122–34
  see also Witnesses

Facts, 73, 75
Fairness, 1–4
  of adversary system of justice,
    52–55
  and morality, 22–23, 24
  of trial(s), 73–74
Fall River Globe (newspaper), 30
Federal Bureau of Investigation,
    Index of Crime, 136

Felonies, 3, 23
Fincher, E.B.:
  American Legal System, The,
    55
Fisch, Isidor, 100, 104, 107
Fish, Albert, 21
Fisher, C. Lloyd, 99, 103
Foreignness:
  and belief in culpability, 40–
    51, 100, 105, 108
Foster, Jodie, 123, 125–26, 127,
    129, 130
Frankfurter, Felix, 48, 49

Gacy, John Wayne, 111–21,
    133
Galloway, Scotland, 5–11
Galsworthy, John, 48
Garfield, James, 136
Garippo (judge in Gacy case),
    117, 118, 121, 133
Gerber, Samuel R., 79–80, 81,
    82
Grand jury(ies), 25, 33–34, 43,
    44
Guilt, 24–25, 135, 139
  inequality and determination
    of, 54–55
  insanity and, 135–38
Guilty but mentally ill (verdict),
    133, 137
Guiteau, Charles, 136

Hanley, Jack, *see* Gacy, John
    Wayne
Hanley, James, 115
Harvard University, Medical
    College, 59, 60, 61
Hauptmann, Anna, 96, 98, 103
Hauptmann, Manfred, 96

Hauptmann, Richard Bruno, 95–108
Hayes, Susan, 81, 83
Hearsay, 74
Hearst papers, 97–98
Hill, Charles, 114
Hinckley, John W., Jr., 122–34
Hinckley trial:
    and insanity defense, 136–38
Hoffman, Harold, 103–04, 105, 106, 107–08
Hopper, John, 125, 126
Houk, John Spencer, 78
Houk, Mrs. John, 78

Illinois law, 121
Illinois Supreme Court, 121
Indictment(s), 33, 43
Inequality(ies):
    and determination of guilt, 54–55
Inference, 75
Innocence, presumption of, 52, 54, 109
Insanity defense, 118, 119, 135–38
    Hinckley, 127–28, 129, 130–31, 132–34
    proposed legislation re, 137
"Irresistible impulse" (insanity defense), 136, 137

James VI, King of Scotland (also James I of England), 5, 8
Jews, 109
Johnson, Mrs. Simon, 40–41, 46
Johnson, Simon, 40, 45, 46
Judge(s), 52, 74, 76, 108, 133
    abuse of power by, 52, 53

charge to jury, 35–36, 38, 46, 53, 63, 75, 100–101, 103, 119, 121, 130–31
    and protection of accused, 54
    in Roman law, 54
"Judgement of God," 25
Jurors, motives of, 53
Jury(ies), 3–4, 23, 76, 109, 139
    Gacy case, 117, 119, 120, 121
    Hinckley case, 129, 130–31, 133
    Lindbergh case, 97, 98, 100–101, 103
    Lizzie Borden case, 34, 35–36
    Parkman case, 75
    Sacco-Vanzetti case, 44, 48
    Sheppard case, 83, 85
    unanimity of vote, 53
    Wallace case, 70
Jury system, 24, 25, 52–55, 87
Justice:
    adversary system of, 52–53
    as social goal, 139–40
    struggles for, 55
Juvenile delinquency, 55

Katzmann, Frederick G., 44, 45
Keep, Nathan, 63
Kidnappings, 98
    Lindbergh baby case, 89–108
Kirk, Paul Leland, 85, 86, 88

Law(s):
    criminal, 3
    effectiveness of, 139–40
    evolution of, 23
    place, time, and, 21–25

Law enforcement, 23, 24
Lawyers, 3, 76
  defense, 25
  and fairness, 53
  objections to evidence, 73–74
Legal system:
  questions about, 139
  see also Criminal justice system
Lennon, John, 126, 129
Lewis, Sinclair, 48
Lies, lying in trials, 107
Lindbergh baby kidnapping, 89–108, 109
Lindbergh, Charles A., 89, 91, 92–94, 103, 106
Listalot (co.), 125
Littlefield, Ephraim, 61–62, 63

McCarthy, Timothy, 122
Mann, Thomas, 48
Mass murder:
  Gacy case, 111–12, 116, 117, 120
Massachusetts law, 32, 34, 49
Medeiros (member of Morelli gang), 49
Media, 109, 139
  trial by, 77–78
  see also Press
Mens rea test (insanity defense), 137, 138
Mercurio, El (newspaper), 18
Michigan, 138
Millay, Edna St. Vincent, 48
Misdemeanors, 23
M'Naghten, Daniel, 135
M'Naghten rule, 135, 136, 137, 138

Mob(s), 43, 48, 139
  trial by, 89–108, 109
Morality:
  of cannibalism, 17–18
  and law, 4, 138
  time, place, and, 22–23, 24
Morse, John Vinnicum, 26, 27, 28, 31
Motive(s):
  of jurors, 53
  Lizzie Borden case, 31, 32, 35
  Wallace case, 69, 70, 72
Murder weapon(s), 73
  Lizzie Borden case, 32, 33, 34
  Wallace case, 69, 72

Nazi Germany, 109
Necessity (legal defense), 21–22
New Jersey law, 97, 100, 105
New York State, 138
Nonviolent crime(s), 138

Oath(s), 24

Paez, Carlitos, 15
Pardon(s), posthumous, 47, 51
Parkman, George, 56–65, 75
Parks, John, 72
Parrado, Fernando, 12–14, 15, 16–17
Parry, Reginald Gordon, 72
PDM (Painting, Decorating, and Maintenance) (co.), 112–13, 115–16, 117
Peel, Sir Robert, 135
Perez, Marcelo, 15, 16
Perjury, 45

Petit jury, 33
    see also Jury(ies)
Piest, Robert, 113, 115, 116
Place:
    and right and wrong, 21–25
Police:
    Gacy case, 112–13, 115, 118
    in Lindbergh baby kidnapping, 89, 90, 91–92, 94, 95–97, 98, 99, 105, 106
    see also Evidence technicians (ETs)
Political activity:
    and belief in culpability: Sacco-Vanzetti, 43, 45–46, 48–49, 50–51, 53
Poverty:
    and determination of guilt, 55
Premeditation, 64
Press (the), 42, 118
    in Lindbergh case, 91, 97–98, 107
    see also Media
Process schizophrenia, 128
Prosecution, 3, 52
    Gacy case, 117–18, 119, 120–21
    Hinckley case, 128–31
    in insanity cases, 137
    Lindbergh case, 98–99, 100, 105
    Lizzie Borden case, 34, 35, 36
    Parkman case, 62
    Sacco-Vanzetti case, 44, 45–46, 48, 52, 53
    Sheppard case, 82, 86–87
    Wallace case, 69
Psychiatrists, 127–29, 130, 137

Public (the):
    and justice, 109–10
    see also Mob(s)
Public opinion, 82
Publicity, pretrial, 117
Punishment, 3, 11, 23

Qualtrough, R.M., 67, 68, 69

Ransom money, Lindbergh case, 90, 92, 93, 94–96, 99, 100, 104, 106, 108
Reagan, Ronald, 122, 127, 130, 134, 137
Real evidence, 73, 74
Reasonable doubt, 3, 52, 63, 70
Regina v. Dudley and Stephens, 22
Reilly, Edward J., 98, 99, 103
Right and wrong:
    knowledge of, 10, 11
    time, place, and, 22–23, 24
    see also Morality
Rights:
    of society vs. individual, 138
    see also Constitutional rights
"Right-wrong" test (insanity defense), 135–36, 137
Rigor mortis, 70
Roman Catholic Church:
    stand on cannibalism, 17–18, 20
Roman law, 53–54
Roosevelt, Franklin D., 95, 104

Sacco, Nicola, 41–51, 52, 53
St. Johns, Adela Rogers, 97–98
Salsedo, Andrea, 43, 45
Sanity/insanity issue, 110, 135–38

Sanity/insanity issue (*cont'd*)
  Gacy, 112, 115, 116–19
  Hinckley, 123, 127–29
  see also Insanity defense
Scaduto, Anthony:
  Scapegoat, 104, 105, 106–7, 108
Scapegoat(s), 108, 109
Scapegoat (Scaduto), 104
Scotland, 22
Secret Service, 122–23
Seltzer, Louis B., 80–81, 82, 85
Sentencing, 49–50, 103, 120–21, 133
Sequestering of jury, 97
Serda, Armando, 13–14
Sexual prejudice in determination of guilt, 55
Shaw, Lemuel, 63, 75
Sheppard, Chip, 79
Sheppard, Marilyn, 77, 78, 85–87
Sheppard, Richard, 78, 79
Sheppard, Sam, 77–88, 109
Sheppard, Stephen, 79
Sinclair, Upton, 48
Smith, William French, 137
Society(ies):
  decide right and wrong, 23
  and Hinckley verdict, 136, 137
  and insanity defense, 138
  insanity in, 109, 110
  justice as goal of, 139–40
  and persons accused of violent crimes, 3
  represented by prosecution, 52
  resolution of tensions through laws, 21–25
  rights of, 137, 138

South Braintree, Mass., 40
Strauch, Adolfo, 15
Sullivan, Bridget, 26, 27, 28–29, 30, 31, 32
Survival cannibalism, 22, 23, 24
  see also Cannibalism
Sweeney Todd (musical), 21

Taboo(s), 20
Taxi Driver (book), 123
Taxi Driver (film), 124, 125, 128, 129
Television as witness to murder, 122–34
Testimony, 73, 74
  Lindbergh case, 106
  Lizzie Borden case, 26, 30–32, 34, 36, 38
  Sacco-Vanzetti case, 45, 49
  Sheppard case, 82
  see also Expert testimony
Thayer, Webster, 44, 46, 48, 49, 50
Time:
  and right and wrong, 21–25
Tindal, Lord Chief Justice (Eng.), 135
Trenchard (judge, Lindbergh case), 100–101, 103
Trial(s), 25
  by battle, 25
  fairness of, 73–74
  Gacy, 117–19
  Hinckley, 122, 127–30
  by jury, 3
  Lindbergh case, 107
  Lizzie Borden, 34–35, 38, 53
  by media, 77–88
  by mob, 89–108
  by ordeal, 24–25

Trial(s) (cont'd)
Parkman case, 62
in Roman law, 54
Sacco-Vanzetti case, 43, 44, 52, 53
Sheppard case, 81–83
Tukey (Boston city marshal), 58, 60, 65

United States:
"deportation delirium," 42–43
laws re cannibalism, 21–22
U.S. Attorney General, 42
U.S. Congress:
hearings on insanity defense, 137, 138
Senate, Subcommittee on Criminal Law, 133
U.S. Constitution, 42
U.S. Department of Justice, 42
U.S. Supreme Court, 87, 121
U.S. v. Holmes, 21–22
Uruguayan rugby team, 12–20, 22–23, 24

Vanderbilt Energy Corporation, 124
Vanzetti, Bartolomeo, 41–51, 52, 53
Vengeance, private, 3
Verdict(s), 4, 76
cannibalism case: Uruguayan rugby team, 19–20
finality of, 54
Gacy case, 120–21
Hinckley case, 131, 132–34, 137

Lindbergh case, 102–8
Lizzie Borden case, 37–39
Parkman case, 63, 64–65
Sacco-Vanzetti case, 47–51
Sawney Beane Family cannibalism case, 11
Sheppard case, 84–88
Wallace case, 71–72
Violence, lawful, 110
Violent crime(s), 3, 136
insanity defense in, 137–38
"Voice of common fame," 25

Wallace, Julia, 66–67, 68, 69, 72
Wallace, William Herbert, 66–72, 76
Washington, D.C., 136
Waterloo (Iowa) Jaycees, 114
Webster, John White, 60–61, 62, 63, 64–65, 75
Wells, H. G., 48
Wendel, Paul H., 104, 105, 106, 108
Wilentz, David, 98–99, 103, 104–05, 108
William Brown (ship), 22
Wiretapping, 73
Witnesses, 24, 33, 73, 74
Lizzie Borden case, 26, 34, 38, 39
Sacco-Vanzetti case, 40, 44–45
Sawney Beane Family cannibalism case, 7
Wallace case, 67–68, 70, 72
see also Eyewitness(es)
Woman as murderer, 26–39, 53, 54–55